T. W. Smith BA

Brodie's Notes on William Shakespeare's

Julius Caesar

Pan Books London and Sydney

First published by James Brodie Ltd
This edition published 1976 by Pan Books Ltd
Cavaye Place, London SW10 9PG
          13 14 15 16 17 18 19 20
© T. W. Smith 1976
ISBN 0 330 50004 X
Filmset in Great Britain by
Northumberland Press Ltd, Gateshead, Tyne and Wear
Printed and bound by
Richard Clay (The Chaucer Press) Ltd, Bungay, Suffolk

Contents

To the student

A close reading of the play is the student's primary task,
but it is well worth seeing a performance if possible.
These Notes will help to increase your understanding and
appreciation of the play, and to stimulate *your own* thinking
about it: *they are in no way intended as a substitute* for a
thorough knowledge of the play.

The author and his work

Surprisingly little is known of the life of our greatest dramatist, and the little we can be sure about comes mainly from brief references to him in legal or other formal documents. Though there is no record of Shakespeare's actual birth date, we do know that he was christened William at the market town of Stratford-on-Avon on 26 April 1564. He was the third child of John Shakespeare – variously described as glover, wool dealer, farmer and butcher – and Mary Arden, whose family were prosperous local landowners. However, until the year 1578, when his business began to decline, John Shakespeare was a notable figure in Stratford, and William was probably educated at the local grammar school – where he would have learned the 'small Latin and less Greek' of which the playwright Ben Johnson (1572–1637) accused him. But John Aubrey (1626–97) in his *Brief Lives* (written in the seventeenth century but not published until 1813) says that Shakespeare had 'enough education to become a schoolmaster' – and stated categorically that his father was *not* a butcher.

In 1582, at the age of eighteen, Shakespeare married Anne Hathaway, a woman eight years his senior, who bore him two girls and a boy: Susanna in 1583 and the twins Hamnet and Judith in 1585. He is thought to have left Stratford for London in 1585: there is a tradition (which Aubrey does not deny) that Shakespeare had to flee his native town to avoid prosecution for stealing deer in Sir Thomas Lucy's grounds. But, more to the point, it seems that he left with a band of strolling players, the Queen's Players, who visited Stratford in 1585.

Whether he took his wife and children with him to London is not known, but a pamphlet published in 1592 by a lesser playwright Robert Greene mentions Shakespeare as an actor and playwright. Plague caused the theatres to close in 1593; on their reopening in the following year we know that Shakespeare was by then a member of The Lord Chamberlain's Company (known after the accession of James I as The King's Men). It is probable that he stayed with this company throughout the remainder of his career, writing plays and acting in them in various theatres. His connection with the company must have brought him considerable financial reward, and Shakespeare seems to have been a good businessman as well, for when he retired to Stratford in 1611, aged forty-seven, he was already a fairly wealthy man and a shareholder in two theatres, the Globe and the Blackfriars. He purchased New Place, one of the largest houses in Stratford – where he entertained Ben Jonson and the poet Michael Drayton (1563–1631), and – by the astute purchase of tithes and arable land – he became, in the tradition of his maternal forefathers, a prosperous landowner. He died in Stratford-on-Avon on 23 April 1616, survived by his wife and two daughters.

As an actor Shakespeare does not seem to have been particularly successful; but even in his own day his fame as a dramatist and his personal popularity were great. In 1598 Francis Meres (1565–1647), the writer of critical assessments of playwrights, described Shakespeare as 'the most excellent in both kinds' [i.e. in comedy and in tragedy], and even Ben Jonson, whose dramatic work was in a very different vein, remarks of Shakespeare in *Discoveries* (posthumously published in 1640), 'I lov'd the man and do honour his memory (on this side idiolatry) as much as any.' And John Milton (1608–74) wrote in his poem 'l'Allegro' (1632) the often-quoted lines: 'Or sweetest Shakespeare fancy's child/Warble his native woodnotes wild.'

Shakespeare probably began his work as a dramatist by collaborating with others and patching up old plays for his company to revive. His first completely original play is believed to be *Love's Labour's Lost* (?1590), though the date of each play presents a problem: the dates are not given in the First Folio (the first collected edition of his plays, 1623). His first narrative poems, composed during the Plague when the theatres were closed, were *Venus and Adonis* (1593) and *The Rape of Lucrece* (1594). His 154 *Sonnets* were published in 1609 – without Shakespeare's permission, it is said. The first 126 of these intensely personal poems are addressed to a young man, the poet's friend and patron; the remainder to a 'dark lady'. The identity of neither of these two inspirers of the sonnets has been established – nor has it been decided how far the series is autobiographical.

Most of the plays were written for performance in the public playhouses, and were conveniently classified in the First Folio in three groups: comedies, histories and tragedies. But these divisions are too arbitrary – the 'comedies' can contain tragedy, the 'tragedies' moments of mirth, and the histories have aspects of both tragedy and comedy.

When, however, the plays are considered chronologically they fall naturally into four periods. From about **1590–93** Shakespeare was **learning his trade** while patching up existing plays and beginning to write his own: to this period belong *Love's Labour's Lost*, *The Comedy of Errors*, *Two Gentlemen of Verona*, the three *Parts* of *Henry VI*, *Romeo and Juliet* and *Richard III*.

From about **1594–1600** was the period of Shakespeare's **greatest development**, when he wrote such plays as *Titus Andronicus*, *A Midsummer Night's Dream*, *The Merchant of Venice*, *The Taming of the Shrew*, the two *Parts* of *Henry IV*, *The Merry Wives of Windsor*, *As You Like It* and *Twelfth Night*.

Despite what we have said above, the period **1602–08** can be described as that of **the tragedies**, which include *Hamlet*, *Othello*, *King Lear*, *Macbeth* and *Antony and Cleopatra*.

Shakespeare's **final period (1610–13)** includes three romances: *The Tempest*, *Cymbeline* and *The Winter's Tale*; and one historical play, *Henry VIII*.

As for the original productions of these plays, Shakespeare cared little about the dress of his characters – irrespective of place or period, the actors wore the English fashions of his time. And whatever might be a play's geographical setting, his clowns and lower-class characters were true London cockneys or British country bumpkins – such as would appeal to the gallery in English playhouses.

Since that time, there have been many fashions in 'dressing' the plays: there have been attempts at contemporaneous setting and clothes – in more recent times some of the plays have been produced against stark backgrounds and in modern dress. But today there is a movement towards vaguely 'historical' dress, and (after decades of sonorous, sometimes pompous and often unintelligible speaking of the lines) to the simpler, more naturalistic delivery, such as Shakespeare's original players probably used. But, notwithstanding the many and various innovations over the years, Shakespeare's genius, his lyrical lines and wonderful choice of words, his warmth and his understanding of the human predicament, continue to bring entertainment and enlightenment to people all over the world.

The Elizabethan Theatre

At the time of Shakespeare there were probably not more than five public theatres in the land, all in London, and they were built according to the design of the inn-yards of the period, which had been found marvellously convenient places for the presentation of plays.

The theatre was circular or octagonal in shape. The main part of the auditorium was the large round pit, open to the sky, in which the poorer people *stood* (the 'groundlings'). Encircling this, round the walls, were three balconies, covered on top but not in front (like the 'stands' on a football ground), and containing seats. The price of admission to the pit was one penny, worth nearly 10p today, and balcony seats ranged from twopence to half a crown (20p to £3), according to their position. When it was wet the performance was postponed until the next day.

The stage was large, which made it easy to show crowd and battle scenes, as in *Julius Caesar*. It jutted far into the pit; hence it made no difference that people stood at the side of the stage as well as in front. It was without scenery and any but the most meagre properties. The scenery was created in the imagination of the audience by the words of the characters in the play, so as not to obtrude and destroy the illusion of reality, as, for example, at the beginning of I,3, II,1, and V,1. *Julius Caesar*, so much of which happens at night, would be performed in broad daylight. The audience is made aware of the imaginative setting, so different from the actual setting when the play was produced, by little natural touches in the dialogue, as in I,3 and II,1. In the latter scene, too, the references to the storm help to keep it ever before the audience.

The play went straight on without intervals. Lack of intervals and frequent changes of scene were immaterial when the stage was without scenery, consequently a succession of short scenes, as in Act V, is quite common in Elizabethan drama.

In the early part of the present century Shakespeare's plays were presented with elaborate scenery, and sometimes the audience would become impatient at the constant delays while it was being changed. At the present time there is a return to a simple stage setting, in

keeping with that of Shakespeare's day, as, for instance, at the Royal Shakespeare Theatre, Stratford-on-Avon. There is good reason to believe that when they were first produced the plays took considerably less time than they do today. The Prologue to *Romeo and Juliet*, for instance, refers to 'the two hours' traffic of our stage'.

The end of a scene was frequently marked by rhyming lines, as at the end of Act I, Sc.2, or at the deaths of Titinius and Brutus in Act V, Scenes 3 and 5 respectively. With regard to the latter, remember that Shakespeare did not divide his plays into acts and scenes (see p.11) and that what seems the end of only a part of a scene, as printed in our editions, may well have appeared the end of a separate scene to him, as here.

Just as the scenery had to be *put into* the words of the play, so had entrances and exits to be arranged as *part of* the play. In a modern play an actor can get into position before the rise of the curtain, but on the open stage it would seem artificial if he walked on and then started his first speech, or finished the scene and then walked off. Such endings as II,1, 'Follow me then', clear the stage and at the same time fit in perfectly with the action of the play. It follows that dead bodies always have to be carried off the stage in the action of the play, as in III,1, 'Lend me your hand'.

It was not unknown for the stage floor to be equipped with a trap-door for the sudden appearance and disappearance of ghosts and spirits, and some theatres had a flying apparatus by which such could descend on the stage with the aid of ropes on runners. Under the stage was the orchestra, a very important feature of the Elizabethan theatre.

At the back of the stage was a recess 'within', and this was curtained and could be shut off when desired. The recess might be used in IV,1, where the three triumvirs are seated at a table. Above the recess was a balcony, which served for an upper room, castle walls, and such scenes. This, too, could be curtained off.

The young 'bloods' of the day who fancied themselves actually hired stools round the stage itself. It was a source of continual annoyance to playwrights that actors 'gagged' in order to please these aristocratic playgoers.

By law, no women were allowed to act. Consequently women's parts were taken by boys with unbroken voices. Imagine a boy's rendering of Lady Macbeth or Imogen or Cleopatra! This accounts for the few women's parts in plays of the period, though some were always introduced for the sake of variety. It also accounts for the large number of plays where a woman disguises herself as a page boy. It made it much easier for the producer; further, the audience was intrigued by a situation in which a character was pretending to be what he really was.

Plays were not acted in period costume. Thus all Shakespeare's plays were first acted in 'modern dress'. In considering their suitability for presentation in modern dress today, however, it must not be forgotten that the language of the plays fits in with the Elizabethan costume worn by the actors originally. Although there was no scenery, managers spared no expense on the most lavish of costumes.

On days when the theatre was open a flag was flown from the turret, and when the play was about to begin a trumpet was sounded.

The text of Shakespeare's plays

Few readers of Shakespeare realize the difficulties scholars have had to overcome in order to establish accurate texts of the plays. The First Folio (see p.6) contained thirty-six plays. Other collected editions or Folios were published in the seventeenth century, the Third and Fourth Folios containing seven additional plays, none of which, with the exception of *Pericles*, is now thought to be by Shakespeare. Sixteen of the plays had already been published separately as Quartos before 1623, and in the case of some plays, for example, *Hamlet*, more than one Quarto edition exists. Some of these Quartos are almost word for word the same as the texts in the First Folio and were possibly set up from Shakespeare's own manuscript or at least from accurate theatre copies; but others are shortened, inferior versions, possibly 'pirated' editions published by some unauthorized person who had access to theatre copies or parts of them, or who had taken down the plays in shorthand while they were being performed. It is thought that the texts of the First Folio were set up from the good Quartos and from good theatre copies. But these texts must all be compared, printers' mistakes, and other interference traced, before a reliable text can be arrived at. Such a task has been unnecessary in the case of *Julius Caesar*, as the first known edition is that of the First Folio, and the text has very few doubtful passages. All the acts of *Julius Caesar* are marked in the First Folio, but no scenes, except Sc.1 at the start, which obviously serves no purpose by itself.

The first editor to attempt the problem of the text was Nicholas Rowe (1674–1718), who also divided most of the plays into acts and scenes, supplied place-names of the location of each scene, indications of entrances and exits and a list of dramatis personae, which are absent from many of the texts in the Quarto and Folio editions. Rowe's divisions are convenient for reference (like the divisions of the books of the Bible into chapters and verses) but have no important use in Shakespearean study. They were fitted for the stage of his time, but were unnecessary upon Shakespeare's stage with the barest of scenery.

While knowledge of the text is important for examination study, it should never be forgotten that the literary aspect is more vital.

Title, plot and source

Title

Brutus has all the characteristics of a tragic hero. A noble character stoops to conspiracy and, by errors of judgement, the product of his unpractical idealism, brings on himself and others defeat and death. Why not, then, *The Tragedy of Brutus*? Caesar dies half-way through the play and Brutus receives the final tribute.

The answer to that question must be put briefly. This, the first of the Roman plays, follows closely on the English Histories, in which the monarch gives his name to the drama enacted in his reign, however great or small the part he plays in it. What more natural than that the Roman dictator should follow suit? The suggestion may be added that, just as the Roman citizens were more affected than anything else by Caesar's 'poor dumb mouths', so the main thing for which an Elizabethan audience would assemble would be to see 'Caesar bleed in sport'.

Moreover, the choice is justified structurally. The balance of the plot gives no one of the chief characters, not even Brutus, absolute predominance over the others. The central theme, and the climax, is the assassination of Julius Caesar. The first two acts are concerned with the preparation, the last two with the retribution. It is interesting to note here that Plutarch's *Life of Julius Caesar* ends with the suicide of Brutus.

Further, Caesar's influence is felt even more powerfully after his death than in his life: as Brutus says (V,3,94), 'O Julius Caesar! thou art mighty yet!' And at the end the imperial crown is secured to Octavius.

Plot

The popular dictator, Julius Caesar, is celebrating a triumph, but republican partisans are secretly opposed to his growing power, and there intrudes upon the scene of pomp and splendour the mysterious warning, 'Beware the Ides of March'.

The fears of Brutus, a noble Roman, are played upon by Cassius, who envies Caesar his greatness, and his arguments are reinforced by Casca's account of the offer of a crown to the dictator, who, however, has refused it out of regard for popular feeling, which hates the name of king.

That night, a stormy one full of portents, Cassius gathers his band of conspirators. The meet at the house of Brutus, whom they mean to choose as leader because of his reputation for honesty. Accepting leadership, Brutus forces his decisions upon the others, deciding that Caesar only shall be killed.

The next morning, the Ides of March, Caesar is reluctant to go to the meeting of the Senate owing to his wife's dream, but is persuaded to appear by Decius, one of the conspirators. When Caesar has taken his seat, the whole band press round him in support of a petition they know he will refuse. At a given signal they all stab him and proclaim liberty to a Senate which flees in a body.

Caesar's lieutenant, Antony, who has been detained from the meeting, appears under a safe-conduct and secures from Brutus permission to deliver a public oration at Caesar's funeral, promising to throw no blame on the conspirators. Speaking after Brutus, he keeps to the letter of his promise, until the crowd understand his ironical references to the 'honourable men', and, enraged by the spectacle of Caesar's scarred corpse and urged by the generous terms of his will, they riot. Brutus and Cassius flee from Rome.

Antony, Lepidus (another general) and young Octavius, Caesar's heir, draw up a black-list of their enemies, but meanwhile Brutus and Cassius have raised armies in the East. A bitter quarrel between these two is followed by a reconciliation, but fate seems against them. Brutus, oppressed by a visit from Caesar's ghost, is impatient to settle the issue with Antony and Octavius on the plains of Philippi. His wing is victorious over Octavius, but Cassius, defeated by Antony, kills himself under a misapprehension. The conflict is renewed, and this time Brutus is driven from the field to commit suicide in his turn. The spirit of Caesar is avenged.

A famous and rather complicated period of Roman history has been skilfully condensed into a plot which is one of the best-constructed among Shakespeare's plays. The issue is clear-cut, and the action moves forward unhasting, but with a fatal sureness, to a predestined end.

An unusually large number of *dramatis personae* are carefully grouped and disposed of, the chief characters being subtly contrasted. Historical intervals are drastically cut down, without, however, leaving any noticeable gap in the structure. The opening lines of the scenes in this play are particularly worth study, because of their effectiveness in smoothing the transition from one event or place to another.

Source

Julius Caesar, like its sequel *Antony and Cleopatra* and that other Roman tragedy, *Coriolanus*, in which the citizens figure even more prominently, was taken from Sir Thomas North's version of Plutarch's *Lives*, in particular those of *Julius Caesar*, *Marcus Brutus* and *Marcus Antonius*. All three have been drawn upon.

Plutarch, a Greek student of Roman history, who died *c*.140 AD, produced a number of *Parallel Lives*, Greek and Roman heroes being paired off (Caesar is matched with Alexander the Great, Brutus with a philosopher who expelled a tyrant and Antony with a dissipated adventurer of military genius). Plutarch was less interested in historical accuracy than the bearing of character upon destiny, which has given an appeal for all time to his stories. However, it was Shakespeare's genius that created live human beings in *Julius Caesar*, often from mere random hints and references.

Whereas Shakespeare has followed the *Lives* more closely than he did Holinshed, upon whom he drew for his English historical plays (much of the play, indeed, is Plutarch dramatized), yet he made certain alterations, chiefly in the interests of unity of action.

1 The triumph in October, 45 BC, and the Feast of the Lupercalia in February, 44 BC, are combined on one day, apparently 14 March.
2 On the *next* day, 15 March, i.e. 'The Ides of March', the assassination, the funeral (actually two days later) and the arrival of Octavius (in May) all take place.
3 The will, in Plutarch made public *before* the funeral, is read by Antony, over Caesar's body.
4 The greatest simplification of all is that the Triumvirate, who did not meet till October of the following year at Bologna, after months of civil war among themselves, begin their proscription and campaign as if fresh from executing Caesar's will.
5 The quarrels between Brutus and Cassius are composed in one grand reconciliation.

6 Two battles at Philippi, separated by twenty days (the spirit appearing again on the eve of the second), are condensed into two actions on the same day.

The student will notice how often, where Shakespeare might have safely invented for himself, he has 'lifted' whole incidents, as well as ideas and expressions, straight into his play. This is particularly noticeable in Act V, where there is little scope for the 'alchemy' of poetry in the bustle of action. Where he has deviated in matters of detail from the original work, the intention has been to stress some feature in one of his characters.

1 Brutus is given the credit of requiring no oath.

2 Marcellus and Flavius are executed instead of merely losing their office as tribunes – the act of a 'tyrant'.

3 Cicero (at the height of his fame) is used in a minor role, mainly as a foil to Casca, while the Senate appear once only in a very supernumerary capacity.

4 Caesar acquires a touch of nobility by rejecting Artemidorus's petition, instead of being prevented from reading it.

5 Instead of the conspirators being given a safe-conduct from the Capitol, it is Antony who ventures forth and shows his resourcefulness.

6 In Plutarch, Caesar's funeral was according to custom, not an act of grace on the part of Brutus, whose speech was actually made immediately after the assassination and received in silence.

7 The poet's intrusion does not break off the quarrel between Brutus and Cassius, as in Plutarch, but comes as a comic interlude after their *better natures* have surmounted their differences.

8 By the confrontation of the leaders in V,1, the issue is made clear in the minds of the audience; in reality Octavius was absent, sick, and Antony, caught in a tight corner, arrived after his soldiers had won.

9 The vein of cruelty in Cassius is emphasized by his *killing* his standard-bearer.

10 Pindarus, not his short-sighted master, misunderstands the alighting of Titinius, but his description of what he sees serves in the play to inform the audience.

11 The Portia of history took her own life *after* her husband's death.

Theme, setting and style

Theme

Shakespeare's idea of good government was probably a benevolent autocracy. Rulers might have their weaknesses, but violent revolt against the established order generally brought untold suffering and defeated its own ends.

Brutus sought to restore freedom to a people incapable of preserving law and order without a strong ruler. Idealism, too, is admirable in itself, but any important enterprise, whether honourable or dishonourable, requires shrewd dealing, as that English queen knew, who was just drawing to the close of a very astute reign.

Contemporary politics may provide interesting parallels (such as the question of Elizabeth's successor, the plots against her life and the behaviour of the London populace), but they have probably little or nothing to do with the construction of the play. Shakespeare was more interested in the dramatic presentation of a famous assassination and in the motives and blunders of the conspirators. This piece of treacherous mass-stabbing had to be enacted on the stage in full view of the audience, simply because it was familiar to them from their own reading. As if to avoid an anti-climax after the horror of this deed, the playwright made of Brutus a character of more enduring interest than his historical counterpart: an idealist torn between personal loyalty and philosophical principle, who strikes a foul blow in what is for him a noble cause and yet persists in honourable gestures that bring disaster on him and his associates.

Honour surrounds Brutus like an aura, and this might seem to be the theme of the play: a lofty moral outlook with a bookish background, divorced from practical common-sense in dealing with others, leads to tragic failure, as do ambition, jealousy and other human weaknesses in Shakespeare's greatest plays. An exaggerated sense of honour is a dangerous defect in a conspirator, especially a leader in a conspiracy. There are variations on this theme worth noticing.

Taking his cue from Brutus, Cassius declares honour to be the 'subject' of his interview with him; later, after having enlarged to his friend on the dishonourable kind of existence led in the shadow of such a man as Caesar, he remarks to himself how easily Brutus's honourable metal may be twisted out of shape; he introduces Casca to an enterprise which has become to him one of 'honourable-dangerous consequence'.

After listening (off-stage) to Brutus's speech, Antony also uses this declared honour of Brutus with skilful irony, each repetition increasing in severity, until he brands the whole group as 'traitors'. This is, in fact, the climax of the play: Caesar's death was not problematic, while the attitude of the mob was critical.

In the last encounter the death of Brutus is tinged with supreme honour: at first, to die on his sword would confer honour on the victim; then it is vital to his friends that no one should gain honour by slaying Brutus or capturing him alive; finally, the slave who holds the sword is known to his master as having an honourable record!

In the age of conflicting loyalties in which this play of conflicting loyalties was written, the question of personal honour would be of absorbing interest to all immersed in the often treacherous politics under the Tudor dynasty.

Setting

The local colour of all Shakespeare's plays is that of Elizabethan England, whether the story is one of Ancient Rome, Denmark or Egypt, and whatever the period may be. Nowadays we should demand strict accuracy in scenery, costume and topical references, but then, for playwright and audience alike, the life and spirit of a play mattered more than strict accuracy in local colour. People saw in the drama a reflection of their own life and experience; its appeal was in no wise analytical or educational, but human and curiously personal.

Further, in those days people were untravelled and uneducated, and anachronisms would not strike a false note in an age more familiar with the stories than with their settings.

And it must be remembered that there was no scenery and little or no period costume. Thus incongruities which now become apparent would not be noticed then, and references to a character's dress must be to something that he was actually wearing on the stage.

In *Julius Caesar* the conspirators do not draw their togas over their heads, but pull their 'hats' about their ears and bury their faces in their cloaks. Caesar wears a 'doublet', and the sick Caius Ligarius a 'kerchief'. Instead of unrolling his volume, Brutus finds the 'leaf' he has turned down. One of the best known anachronisms is the striking clock in this play. It occurs twice; in each case the hour is by contemporary reckoning, not Roman, and it is Brutus who counts the strokes.

Though differing in detail, festivals, omens, and triumphs would mean much the same thing to Roman and Elizabethan, while the Capitol with its lions approximates to the Tower of London. Casca refers to the 'tag-rag people' clapping and hissing 'the players in the theatre'. The use of Greek by the learned corresponds to that of French among the English educated classes. 'Most horrid sights seen by the *watch*' (the contemporary night-watchman) would have due weight with an audience that went about with a wholesome respect for ghosts, witches, and other night fears.

In spite of the atmosphere of ancient Rome that Shakespeare has created out of the materials from his source, his Caesar subtly suggests some Elizabethan statesman in high office watched enviously by less successful courtiers hoping to bring him down.

Style

Julius Caesar is one of the simplest of Shakespeare's texts to study, manly, lucid and, on occasion, reaching the highest pitch of eloquence. The play contains a large proportion of public orations and private discussions, both highly emotional and making frequent use of hyperbole and irony. As it is concerned with one man who was a world figure and another who was regarded as the soul of honour, exaggeration is inevitable. Since real feelings are constantly being disguised, there are several references to smiles.

Wounded flesh and spouting blood have a special place in the imagery. In the misty half-light of *Macbeth* a blood-stained dagger is a sign of guilt; in *Julius Caesar* a besmeared sword is a sign of liberation. In the former, hands are washed to cleanse them of blood; in the latter, hands are washed in the victim's blood as a ritual act (Shakespeare's idea). To Antony they are still 'bloody fingers', to be shaken in a pretence of friendship until he is in a position to turn the multiple wounds into something different from the life-giving fountain of Decius's interpretation – so many dumb mouths pleading for revenge. Brutus, who 'loved Caesar while he struck', had spared Antony, whom he did not love, to save further bloodshed, and so made possible the revenge, a much bloodier affair.

If Caesar's spirit (in which there was no blood) could have been destroyed without killing his body, Brutus would have been much happier; as it was, he intended the act to be as sacred and restrained as a sacrifice, found consolation in the thought that the dead man need no longer fear death and sought to make of Caesar's life-stream a banner of liberty. In the end the bloodless spirit of the dead dictator looked in at Philippi, we must presume, to see this idealist shed his own blood in defeat.

Use of prose

The normal form of Shakespeare's plays is blank verse. When prose is used, it is for a definite purpose.

Prose is invariably used for

1 Comic characters (e.g. the Cobbler, I,1) and

2 Characters of lower social position (e.g. the Citizens, III,2 and 3).

This was a literary convention at a time when literature was aristocratic and the chief characters in plays (as in life) were kings and nobles. Scenes in which the lower orders of society figure are a contrast; these people live on a lower plane of feeling than the main characters, and thereby emphasize the height of the feeling of the main characters, and the contrast in the medium of expression – prose instead of verse – is in perfect keeping.

3 Letters, formal addresses etc. (e.g. the petition to Caesar).

Prose is also used in this play for purposes of contrast. Brutus's oratorical devices of parallelism, antithesis and climax require prose, while Antony's emotional use of pathos, emphasis, apostrophe, expostulation, and the telling repetition of 'honourable men', finds rhythmical form in verse.

In I,2, Casca alternates the verse queries of the others with a posturing, disjointed prose (suitable to his apparently 'blunt' character). In the very next scene, with sword drawn and staring eyes, he exclaims upon the sights he has seen – in verse. Shakespeare frequently uses his minor characters in this way, to convey information or create atmosphere.

Characters

Julius Caesar

The greatest man of ancient times appears in our play chiefly as an affected autocrat, pretending to a courage and determination he obviously does not possess, superstitious to a degree, and surrounded by obsequious flatterers.

Shakespeare's knowledge of Roman history, derived as it is mainly from Plutarch, was bound to be faulty, but he seems deliberately to have selected the weak points in Caesar's character and omitted any reference to the far-reaching schemes of improvement planned by Caesar. When Shakespeare's Brutus sends Lucius to consult the calendar, no thought crosses his mind that the reformer of that calendar was none other than the great Julius.

There are dramatic reasons for this depreciation of the soldier-statesman: (1) an audience filled with admiration would have been revolted by his killing, especially when it took place on the stage; (2) Brutus would have paled in comparison, and his death would have been less a tragedy than the successful end of a punitive expedition.

Stress had to be laid on Caesar's ambition to be king. He must seem less a great man, more a threat to the liberties of Rome. His will, then, is absolute; the people show their disapproval, but a servile senate is about to gratify him with a crown to be worn outside Italy. Opposition has to be secret and furtive.

Caesar is made to behave as if he were already king. He executes the tribunes for insulting his statues; he issues peremptory commands, listened to in silence and obeyed instantly; he frequently refers to himself in the third person. On the fatal day, the scene at the Capitol takes on the aspect of a court, even before the royal title has been bestowed by the 'graybeards' hovering in the background. Only recently made aware, by Decius Brutus, of the intended honour, and sublimely unaware of what is really intended by the petitioners crouching at his feet, he makes a show of royal authority –

Caesar   *Are we all ready?* What is now amiss
         That Caesar and *his* senate must redress?
Metellus Most high, most mighty, and most puissant Caesar.

If the conspirators lacked any spur to raise their hidden daggers (and in *Plutarch* the magnitude of the deed awes them and makes their first strokes ineffective), it is supplied in the words of the occupant of the golden chair: 'I spurn thee like a cur out of my way', and 'I could be well moved, if I were as you.'

It is no wonder that Cassius describes him as a god before whose nod others must bow, but Casca reports him in a different light when face to face with the citizens. While Caesar sees no harm in telling the Senate the truth – that he simply is not coming – on the other hand, he acts a part before the crowd: he dissimulates his desire for the crown, yet is so cut to the heart by their too enthusiastic applause of his refusal of it, that in a fit he offers them his throat, afterwards apologizing humbly for his strange behaviour.

Physical defects like this seem to justify the otherwise envious speech of Cassius. Casca's account of the epileptic attack reminds us of the same 'fever', whose progress Cassius watched in Spain. The deafness in the left ear which Shakespeare added, he added as an ironic continuation of 'always I am Caesar'.

Other weaknesses are rendered all the more damning (and, incidentally, all the more noticeable) by clumsy attempts to disguise them: 'I rather tell thee what is to fear'd/Than what I fear; for always I am Caesar.' He wished to be thought more dangerous than danger itself. It is impossible he should make a mistake: 'Know, Caesar doth not wrong.' At home his mind is made up for him, first by Calpurnia and then by Decius, yet he would seem inflexible:

But I am constant as the northern star,
Of whose true-fix'd and resting quality
There is no fellow in the firmament.

His love of flattery is concealed from himself:

Decius But when I tell him he hates flatterers,
      He says he does.

His first words on each of his appearances are concerned with superstition: the fertility rites of the Lupercalia, sacrificing for omens, and the soothsayer's warning. In spite of brave words: 'It seems to me most strange that men should fear' – he is much disturbed by Calpurnia's dream and is relieved to have Decius's interpretation of it.

Nevertheless, something finer in the man is discerned in little glimpses, such as the reason for his rejection of Artemidorus's petition: 'What touches us ourself shall be last serv'd', and the good-natured banter with which he, greets his callers. Brutus finds 'no personal cause to spurn at him', though he is perhaps willing to overlook faults in a benefactor.

Caesar, unlike Brutus, possesses some insight into others' characters. Of Cassius he says, 'He is a great observer', and, though he openly dismisses the Soothsayer as a 'dreamer', his secret thoughts are full of the prophecy.

His true greatness, however, is revealed only after his death. In striking him down, Brutus aims at his spirit, but, though he slays the body he cannot destroy that spirit which survives not only in his heirs, but in the more terrible world of the supernatural. Caesar is, indeed, mightier in death than in life. It is as if the manner of his death raises him above all criticism. When he exclaims, 'Hence! wilt thou lift up Olympus?' we still smile at his affectation of greatness; but in a short space we are sobered by the magnitude of the fall.

O mighty Caesar! dost thou lie so low?
Are all thy conquests, glories, triumphs, spoils,
Shrunk to this little measure?

Antony addresses his body as if it can still hear.

O, pardon me, thou bleeding piece of earth,
That I am meek and gentle with these butchers!
Thou art the ruins of the noblest man
That ever lived in the tide of times.

He uses his mantle to recall his brilliant victories as well as to stigmatize individually his murderers; he uncovers his wounds to arouse the pity once felt by Caesar for others; he reads his will to prove he was more generous than ambitious.

Caesar's funeral unleashes the violence of the mob: 'Most noble Caesar, we'll revenge his death.' His ghost is an avenging spirit striking despair into the heart of the least guilty of his slayers: 'O Julius Caesar, thou art mighty yet!' Brutus and Cassius die with his name on their lips.

Brutus

Shakespeare's Caesar covets a kingly crown; his Brutus sets honour above all merely material ambitions. In this man lives – and dies – the last spark of that ancient republican virtue which put public interest before personal advancement, which preserved a sense of dignity and responsibility in the conduct of affairs, which set its face against corruption and luxurious living, and which allowed personal dictatorship only in time of emergency. It is this traditional virtue which, while it leads him to help in assassinating the man who threatens the liberties of the State and then to make decisions which prove fatal to the enterprise, yet commands the respect of his fellows, of the people at large and, in the end, of his enemies. There is no man but honours 'the noble Brutus', but the freedom for which he gives his life is extinct in a generation that must have a Caesar.

Brutus values his honour more than his own safety.

Set honour in one eye and death i' the other,
And I will look on both indifferently.
For let the gods so speed me as I love
The name of honour more than I fear death.

He puts the conspirators on their honour:

What need we any spur but our own cause
To prick us to redress?

He spares Antony, so that their action may seem more honourable, 'We shall be call'd purgers, not murderers.' He bases his claim to a hearing on his reputation: 'Believe me for mine honour, and have respect to mine honour, that you may believe.'

Sooner than the dishonour of going 'bound to Rome', he falls on his sword held by a man whose life has had 'some smatch of honour in it'. Not even defeat can stain 'the even virtue of our enterprise', for, in his own eyes, he falls not as a traitor, but as a martyr in the cause of freedom. As Antony says of him (V,5,68), 'This was the noblest Roman of them all'.

This sense of honour, typical of a philosopher and reputed descendant of the Brutus of the early republic, has two aspects: (1) a virtuous life, (2) loyalty to republican traditions or 'freedom'.

Brutus is outstanding among the characters of the play for his transparent honesty, self-restraint and fortitude. His honesty makes him widely respected: 'O, he sits high in all the people's hearts.' His calmness rarely deserts him: when Popilius Lena speaks to Caesar, Brutus steadies Cassius with a word; when the ghost materializes, he is almost flippant. His Stoicism wrings admiration from his friends: 'Even so great men great losses should endure.'

Brutus loves Caesar, but he loves Rome more, and to him the soul of Rome is that ancient liberty handed down from the days when his ancestor expelled the last of the kings. He cannot see that that liberty has degenerated into licence (represented in the play by popular admiration for favourite generals who pamper the citizens with shows), nor is he capable of foreseeing that, by removing one beneficent despot, he will bring about a worse tyranny. To him the rule of one man reduces the rest to slaves: 'Who is here so base that would be a bondman?' The spectacle of Caesar's quasi-royal power offends him, not because the dictator is an ordinary man (which so enrages Cassius), but because everyone seems to be at his beck and call.

Brutus had rather be a villager
Than to repute himself a son of Rome
Under these hard conditions as this time
Is like to lay upon us.

If Caesar is invested with such authority for life, sheer despotism may result:

The abuse of greatness is, when it disjoins
Remorse from power.

There is in Brutus a touch of personal pride in his reputation for honesty and philosophy. He is 'arm'd so strong in honesty' that he neither fears Cassius's threats nor spares his faults; he 'bears too great a mind' to be taken alive; he even stoops to pretence over the loss of his wife, when, hearing the news for the *second* time, he utters the laconic remark, 'Why, farewell, Portia'.

His scrupulous honesty finds *reasons* to justify every action. Unfortunately these reasons are usually too abstract and unsuited to the circumstances of very real problems. He argues to himself in proverbs: 'It is the bright day that brings forth the adder.'

Caesar has not yet proved himself a tyrant, but he may do so if crowned, so the serpent must be killed in the shell. Or he brings sentiment into the matter. There must be no mangling of Caesar's 'limbs' and, since Caesarism cannot be destroyed without shedding the blood of Caesar, 'Let's carve him as a dish fit for the gods.'

In discussions concerning the omission of an oath, the 'sounding' of Cicero, the question of Antony's fate, permission for Antony to address the crowd, and the march to Philippi, he overbears Cassius with a flood of eloquence based on such abstract reasons as the word of a Roman or the sacred character of their enterprise.

He is so blinded by worship of reason that:

1 He expects it to explain away all opposition – 'Our reasons are so full of good regard/That were you, Antony, *the son of Caesar,*/You should be satisfied.'
2 He believes the citizens will be convinced by logical arguments – 'public reasons shall be rendered/Of Caesar's death.
3 He expects others to yield to him – 'Good reasons must, of force, give place to better.'
4 And therefore he is not easily impressed by the reasoning of others. He seems to lend a more attentive ear to the distant acclamations than to Cassius's long tirade against Caesar; only when his wife reveals her wound is he impressed enough to share his secret with her.

The highest praise he can accord Caesar and the main objection he has to overcome before deciding to act are both simply this – 'I have not known when his affections sway'd/More than his reason.'

Antony seizes on Brutus's devotion to honour and his fetish of reason when, at the funeral, he treats the one with irony and the other with sarcasm: 'they are wise and honourable/And will, no doubt, with reasons answer you.'

The reasons of Brutus, even if all were well-founded, are off-set by a superficial knowledge of men's characters and motives. He sees in Antony merely a reveller; he thinks his accomplices are equally animated with 'pity to the general wrong of Rome'; he looks on the crowd as a body of free citizens capable of forming independent judgements: 'Censure me in your wisdom, and awake your senses, that you may the better judge.'

Taking men at their word, he is too honest to suspect ulterior motives. He trusts Antony to keep his promise not to cast any blame; the applause of the crowd serves only to increase his confidence. All through he fails to see that Cassius is 'humouring' him – using him as a tool for his own ends.

At the very end, Brutus sees the avenging spirit of Caesar as responsible for his disaster, not his own misjudgements or any betrayal of his trust in others, and he dies self-assured that:

My heart doth joy that yet in all my life
I found no man but he was true to me.

This idealism is the offspring of philosophic study. Of Brutus the student we have one brief glimpse in his tent before the fatal battle: while others sleep, he reads on into the night, finding solace in some favourite philosopher. Assassination does not occur to him till he is prompted by Cassius and his 'bills'. The need of the moment seems to call him from more congenial pursuits into the fray of political action. Only Brutus could say:

So are we Caesar's friends, that have abridged
His time of fearing death.

Like Macbeth, though for different reasons, he hopes that his one blow will be enough, that once 'ambition's debt is paid', the rest will be 'Peace, freedom, and liberty'. No further harm is intended; rather is he prepared to accept full responsibility: 'let no man abide this deed,/But we the doers.' The deed is horrible to him; he is the last to strike, and does so only out of a sense of duty and sharing in the act of liberation:

O, that we then could come by Caesar's spirit,
And not dismember Caesar! But, alas,
Caesar must bleed for it!

It is as the high priest of republican freedom, on whose altar ambition has been sacrificed, that he commands: 'Stoop, Romans, stoop,/And let us bathe our hands in Caesar's blood.' It is a crime which he, unlike Macbeth, could not have committed in his own interests. His nature, ordinarily, is full of gentleness and consideration for others. He thinks more of his wife's health than his own; he hastens to assure old Publius that he is quite safe; twice he refrains from waking the sleeping Lucius, and he makes his messengers sleep on cushions in his tent. None but a slave can be persuaded to put his gentle soul out of its misery.

But the murder of Caesar is a crime, and all the more shocking as he is Caesar's 'angel'. His victim dies with his name on his lips.

This contradictory character of gentle murderer, partly explainable as the victory of patriotism over friendship, is also to be accounted for by minor contradictory elements in his nature. Soon after he mockingly bids the 'monstrous visage' of conspiracy to hide itself, he advises the very same conspiracy to 'look fresh and merrily'; after rating Cassius for corrupt methods of acquiring money, he upbraids him for not giving him some of it; although he has scornfully pointed out that the gay Antony is too fond of life to 'take thought and die for Caesar', he coolly tells Antony's servant:

Thy master is a wise and valiant Roman;
I never thought him worse.

Finally, he who had blamed Cato for suicide runs on his own sword.

There is, too, a certain cold aloofness, an air of always being in the right, which exasperates Cassius in particular: 'Brutus, this sober form of yours hides wrongs.' Brutus feels throughout an antipathy to Cassius, or, rather, to Cassius's bad qualities. After the quarrel which arises out of his merciless fault-finding, he forgives calmly where Cassius does impulsively, and then proceeds to brow-beat him once more with reasons.

In the same way he calmly condemns Caesar for what he *may* do, calmly kisses his hand in joint petition, and calmly stabs his mortally wounded benefactor.

The assassination is not without effect upon that nobility which others admire to the end. He becomes superstitious: 'I know my hour is come.' He boasts of his honour: 'Young man, thou couldst not die more honourable'; and finally, with tears in his eyes, begs his friends to kill him.

These are slight defects, however, passing almost unnoticed beside the generous farewell to Cassius and the pathos of his own last words: 'Caesar, now be still:/ I kill'd not thee with half so good a will.'

Antony pays him the finest tribute in the play in his last speech, and Octavius treats his remains 'according to his virtue', surrendering his tent for the night so that they may rest there, 'order'd honourably'.

Cassius

Caius Cassius should have been the leader of the conspiracy. Instead, having organized it and, by his tactful prompting, won over Brutus to give it the character of an honourable enterprise, he resigns the leadership to his fellow praetor. The politician takes second place to the philosopher. Had he had his way with Antony, the story would have ended very differently.

The characters of the two men are in many respects complementary. Cassius lacks the idealism and self-control of Brutus, as Brutus lacks the shrewdness and fervour of Cassius. Just as each has more intimate friendships, Cassius with Titinius, Brutus with Lucilius, so their association is not a happy one. It is to the credit of the hasty Cassius that his forbearance keeps the partnership in being so long, but this self-effacement proves the undoing of them all. Brutus loses some of his nobility when he takes a hand in the other's undertaking, while Cassius, under the influence of a loftier mind, develops the better side of his nature. The man who detests the superiority of Caesar tacitly admits his inferiority to Brutus.

Yet the love of freedom in men like Cassius, though they are envious and 'be never at heart's ease/Whiles they behold a greater than themselves' may be more deep-seated and fervent than that of those who 'love words better' (V,1,28). Like Brutus, having taken his stand, Cassius is not lacking in personal courage.

In Cassius good and weak points are surprisingly blended. He is tactful in his approaches to Brutus and Casca, yet his temper easily gets the better of him. His hearing is acute, but his eye-sight poor: quick to recognize Casca by his voice and Cinna by his gait (i.e. the sound of his footsteps), he is so unable to see at a distance that he trusts to another's eyes in a critical situation, with fatal results. His shrewd knowledge of men is seen when he appeals to the love of freedom in Brutus and to the love of office in Antony; yet he is blind to his own exaggerated sense of wrong; three times he accuses Brutus of wronging him. Beside the gentle Brutus he is harsh and unattractive, but at heart he has a more human, more affectionate, more loyal side (after all Caesar was not Cassius's friend). In response to Brutus's pledge, he cries:

Fill, Lucius, till the wine o'erswell the cup;
I cannot drink too much of Brutus' love.

He is not the villain of the play (if there is one, it is Decius). His tendency is to brood over injustices until he is desperate and scorns the world around him. Rome has 'lost the breed of noble bloods' and, if Caesar is a 'wolf', Romans are 'sheep'. He claims to Brutus that he is different from the usual run of society (I,2,72–8). His bitter tongue turns all things to account – the 'falling sickness' in I,2,258, and the storm in I,3,72.

His shrewd, practical nature foresees the danger in Antony, and when he cannot have his own way and have him murdered too, he tries to pin him down to a definite statement of support or hostility, so that the conspirators may know how they stand with regard to him.

Will you be prick'd in number of our friends,
Or shall we on, and not depend on you?

He has a much greater insight into character than Brutus; for instance, Casca's post of 'bluntness' does not deceive him, and he has a much better idea than Brutus generally how to tackle people – friends and foes. He is not, however, far-seeing enough to realize that though Brutus would give prestige he would bungle the conspiracy. He condones bribery in time of emergency, but, sooner than live in awe of 'so vile a thing as Caesar', he will make it a point of honour to take his own life, which he frequently and in a rather theatrical manner threatens to do.

Just as Brutus the Stoic alters his attitude to suicide, so Cassius the Epicurean, who formerly denied the influence of the supernatural – believing that 'Men at some time are masters of their fates' – comes in the end to look morbidly at the ravens, crows, and kites whose 'shadows seem/A canopy most fatal.'

Envious, cruel, choleric, Cassius has the gift of making friends in greater measure than the calm, gentle, high-souled Brutus. Lucilius is gratified to find Brutus, as he forecast, the same noble self, honoured in death, but Titinius plunges Cassius's sword into his own heart, saying, 'Brutus, come apace,/And see how I regard Caius Cassius.'

Character contrast of Brutus and Cassius

Brutus	Cassius
Student of books	Observer of men
Believes in principle	Guided by personal considerations
Hates tyranny	Hates the tyrant

Habitually calm	Easily alarmed (Popilius Lena)
'Sober'	'Choleric'
Kind (e.g. Lucius)	Cruel (e.g. standard-bearer)
Coldly aloof	Warmly affectionate
Bears sorrow patiently	Resents injuries
Stoic, abhorring suicide	Epicurean, welcoming it
Persuasive	Yields to the personality of Brutus
Unpractical	Shrewd

The errors of Brutus that stand out against the practical advice of Cassius: spares Antony; gives him permission to hold the public funeral; marches to meet the enemy; gives the signal to charge too soon; neglects to come to the help of Cassius.

Mark Antony

The story of Antony is continued in *Antony and Cleopatra*, in which play the 'peevish schoolboy' crushes the 'masker and reveller'. In *Julius Caesar* little is seen or suggested of Antony's military genius, which made him Caesar's second in command, or his self-indulgence which eventually led to his downfall. His part in our play is that of a quick-witted schemer and powerful orator. There is an attractive dash and fire about him which makes him stand out against the calm Brutus and the crafty Cassius. His love of music, plays, and popular festivals (noted by Caesar) is a mask which deceives Brutus:

For he can do no more than Caesar's arm
When Caesar's head is off,

but not Cassius: 'we shall find of him/ A shrewd contriver.'

For his part, indeed, Antony seems to have been quite unsuspicious of foul play. He reassures Caesar, whose sharp eye has detected the look on Cassius's face:

Fear him not, Caesar; he's not dangerous;
He is a noble Roman and well given,

and is easily drawn away by Trebonius.

In the general confusion, however, he escapes to Caesar's house, whence, having possessed himself of the dead man's papers, he ventures forth with the effrontery of the born gambler, staking all on his knowledge of Brutus. First he sends a messenger to Brutus as the new dictator, declaring that, given *reasons*, he will go over to his side. On the strength of Brutus's word of *honour*, he returns to the scenes of the crime and faces the conspirators, an unarmed man amongst armed men, the one hampered by no moral scruples, the many hampered by the moral scruples of their leader.

He feels his way with them exactly as he does later with the crowd. He praises Caesar and he praises the conspirators; one moment he shakes hands with each of the murderers, the next turns aside to weep over the murdered; he speaks slightingly of himself:

My credit now stands on such slippery ground,
That one of two ways you must conceit me,
Either a coward or a flatterer.

His request to be allowed to mourn Caesar in a public speech 'as becomes a friend' seems as guileless as his production of and refusal to read the will.

Left by himself, his pent-up fury breaks out in a hideous prophecy of civil war, even though the issue is still uncertain. There is no acting here. Antony is capable of a personal devotion as great as the devotion of Brutus to an idea. In the next scene he is at his best, ringing the changes on humility, accusation, reminiscence, indignation, pathos, defiance, modesty, rebuke, until he reaches his climax: 'Here was a Caesar! when comes such another?'

Left alone once more, he reveals even more clearly (cf. III,1,292–4) the cunning which has underlain the whole performance:

Now let it work. Mischief, thou art afoot,
Take thou what course thou wilt!

He has of set purpose aroused the populace to fury, and their violent lust for revenge fills him with a fierce joy in the coming destruction: 'Fortune is merry,/And in this mood will give us everything.'

His cunning in flattering Brutus into giving him the fatal permission is as shameless as the cunning of Decius in flattering Caesar into making his fatal appearance at the Capitol.

The proscription scene portrays Antony at his worst, cruel, mercenary, cynical. He ticks off with zest the names of the victims, proceeds to tamper with the will and boasts of the way he exploits Lepidus. (A historical note may be of interest here: fleeing destitute from Octavius, Antony arrived in the camp of Lepidus, where his tongue won for him the soldier's support, with the result that Lepidus was soon commander in name only.)

On the other hand, he can show quite sincere appreciation of others, for, in addition to the reference to Cassius quoted on p.30 he praises the self-sacrifice of Lucilius: 'I had rather have/Such men my friends than enemies.' He gives orders that Brutus shall not be slain; and when Brutus lies before him, he utters a tribute that is one of the finest things in the language.

Antony's speech to the crowd

Disproves Caesar's ambition, but the honourable men must be believed. (Doubts.) He and they loved the great man, but the honourable men must not be wronged; there is a will, but to read it would anger the people against the honourable men. (The people approve the reading of the will; they crowd round him; he is one of them.) He vividly imagines the assassination. (Tears.) He shows them the victim – of *treason*. (Grief and rage.) But they must not mutiny, because there are reasons; he does not wish to incite them; he is only letting the wounds speak for themselves; but if an orator like *Brutus* . . . (Mutiny.) He calls them back to hear the will; there is a bequest for each of them. (Revenge.) There is a bequest also to the city. (Riots.)

Portia

Brutus is matched with a noble wife. Loving and practical, she seeks to share his anxiety as, on the other hand, Caesar's wife seeks to make him share hers. Calpurnia is without any distinctive trait, save that she knows her husband's weakness for disowning fear. She allows herself to be over-ridden, but Portia is determined to share the secret that comes between her and Brutus – out of a desire to help him, not out of idle curiosity – and tests her self-control to prove to him, when other arguments fail, that she can keep it. That she is so upset at Brutus's silence shows that usually Brutus found her worthy to share his secrets. Brutus treats Portia as a companion, whereas Caesar treats Calpurnia as a child to be put in her place. Portia's attempt to find out what is troubling Brutus is worthy of the daughter and wife of Stoics; in fact it is her pride that she is 'so fathered and so husbanded' that gives her added strength and determination.

Like Lady Macbeth, she is bold in her husband's interests and, like her, too, finds afterwards that she has 'a man's mind, but a woman's might'. Her constancy fails at the crisis (just as Lady Macbeth swoons) and nearly betrays the secret so well kept by others. For fear Lucius may have overheard her prayer for success, she pretends to be anxious about a petition and sends the boy on a frivolous errand. The success of her husband's enemies and the suspense of separation make her so desperate that she is deprived of all means of inflicting a really fatal wound on herself, but a woman of her determination cannot be foiled. Far away, her husband's grief is suppressed – an angry scene with Cassius, and then 'to our work alive'.

Portia is not seen after Act II; she is drawing too much interest to herself, whereas it must be focussed on Brutus and Cassius and Antony.

Octavius Caesar

Caesar's heir is a man of few words. When Antony, on the score of being an older man, has his way with Lepidus, he keeps his own counsel, trusting nobody (IV,1,50). It is when the critical battle is about to be joined that he asserts himself (V,1,20). Impatient of 'words before blows', he draws his sword, the sword of 'another Caesar', and finally cuts the argument short with a challenge to the field. His spirit of cold ruthlessness is a foil to Antony's burning vengeance; his final words leave with the audience an impression that the future lies with him.

Minor characters

Other conspirators. A number of embittered aristocrats, remnants of Pompey's party, seek to give their revolt the appearance of a popular movement for freedom. They are too well-known for what they are (I,3,158), so they borrow the name of Brutus, but, though strengthened by his reputation for honesty, they are destroyed through his decisions. Casca, Decius, Cinna, Metellus, Trebonius, and Ligarius play individual parts up to the re-entry of Antony, after which their fates are no longer of dramatic importance.

Casca is a creation of Shakespeare's (in Plutarch he is conspicuous merely for a rather ineffectual first blow). His character is almost chameleon-like in its changes. Appearing first prominent among the flatterers, he later retails the incident of the crown with a cynical indifference that cloaks a real understanding of the issue – 'to my thinking, he would fain have had it'. Cassius detects the 'wit' under the 'rudeness' and encounters him when all his latent superstition has been roused to a frenzy of fear by the storm. The revelation of a desperate enterprise brings out the bold conspirator. He will go as far as any one to ensure success: no 'fleering tell-tale' himself, he is anxious for the oath of secrecy to be sworn, and he gives the pre-arranged signal with fierce determination, 'Speak, hands, for me!' Such is his admiration for Brutus (I,3,157–60) that a word from the latter causes him to contradict himself (II,1,143–53).

Decius is the hypocritical flatterer. Having wound himself into the affections of Caesar, he betrays him by rousing his fear of ridicule. He cunningly thrusts himself in front of Artemidorus, as if aware of the denial in that 'schedule' of the very love he has just professed.

Cinna must have had a rapid 'gait' to deliver all Cassius's papers in the time. His hated name results in the death of an innocent man.

Trebonius is a good conversationalist. Caesar has 'an hour's talk in store' for him, and his ready tongue draws Antony aside. Certain that the reveller will 'laugh at this hereafter', he is surprised to find Antony 'fled to his house amazed'.

Ligarius, rising from a sick-bed, personifies the blind devotion inspired in others by Brutus.

Cicero, though not one of the conspirators, shares their fate. His fiery eyes are the only hint of his fiery speeches against Antony. Shakespeare's reason for his omission is not the caution of an old statesman, but his characteristic determination to have his way. The orator would not relish being 'cross'd in conference' as Cassius is. His philosophic calmness in the storm is a foil to Casca's breathlessness.

Lepidus. If Cassius is to be condemned for turning his friendship with Brutus to his own advantage, what are we to say of Antony's treatment of Lepidus? In history by no means the cipher Shakespeare makes him appear, he merely serves here to illustrate further the more unpleasant side of Antony's character.

Marullus, the more eloquent of the two tribunes, both anticipates and contrasts with Antony in his manner of speaking to the crowd.

Caesar was unfortunate in that so large a conspiracy was not somehow given away. The gipsy-like *Soothsayer* does his best as mouthpiece of the supernatural, and his cryptic warning is followed by a night of terrifying manifestations, but it is the petition of *Artemidorus*, teacher of rhetoric to politicians – a more practical and documented notification of specific danger – that really increases the dramatic tension. In the street the two come together: to Caesar's jaunty greeting the prophet of woe merely makes a sinister rejoinder, whereas Artemidorus does attempt to save the great man's life, only to be out-manoeuvred by Decius (is this wily conspirator aware of the 'dynamite' in the proffered paper?) and dismissed as a madman by a Caesar risen far above petty personal interests.

The Citizens

If Caesar is represented in a bad light, so are the Citizens. There are dramatic reasons for this, too. In Plutarch they respect Brutus but preserve a stony silence, while they howl down Cinna, so, though described as a 'multitude of rakehels of all sorts', they do not swerve from their allegiance to the champion of the popular party, Caesar. In Shakespeare they are as enthusiastic for Brutus at first as they are enraged against him afterwards.

Again, Pompey had actually left the people's cause for the senatorial party, whereas in the first Scene they appear to have easily transferred their affections from one favourite to another. Not only is this scene a preparation for the greater fickleness to follow, but it provides two contrasting examples in the influence of suggestion on the mass mind. The tribunes *rebuke* them for their cruelty:

You blocks, you stones, you worse than senseless things!
O you hard hearts, you cruel men of Rome,
Knew you not Pompey?

And they vanish 'tongue-tied in their guiltiness'. Antony *arouses* them by denying their hard-heartedness:

You are not wood, you are not stones, but men;
And, being men, hearing the will of Caesar,
It will inflame you, it will make you mad,

and they are mad with rage. Similarly with the workings of mass emotion. When made to reflect on the past glories of Pompey, the whole crowd is sad and silent; when made to look on the mangled body of Caesar, it is fierce and violent.

In the great funeral scene itself, the methods of the two orators are in strong contrast. Brutus, speaking in flexible, balanced prose, convinces them that, with Caesar out of the way, they are now all free men. He lectures them on the ambition of Caesar and offers them a place in the new commonwealth. Antony, in the more emotional medium of verse and employing the simplest expressions, seeks to bring home to them the greatness of their loss. He begins as the humblest of citizens who can only feel like them, knows no more than they do, loved Caesar as they did. He comes down from the pulpit and becomes one of them; he weeps and soon they weep; he mourns Caesar and soon they are all mourning Caesar; Caesar was Antony's friend – and Brutus's – and soon he appears their friend as well. In their sorrow and anger they forget the will, just as they forgot Caesar's refusal of the crown when Brutus said he was ambitious; when the great man's friendship takes the very tangible form of seventy-five drachmas, they forget all about the wonderful new commonwealth promised them by Brutus.

Their exclamations show their inability to hold more than one idea in their heads at once. Their unruliness shows their need of a strong man; they can think only in terms of that autocracy which in name they have rejected: 'Let him be Caesar.' Brutus's ideal of freedom is illusory; the people are unfitted for it. They depend on a spokesman or champion, even if it be only a cobbler bandying puns. All they are good at is shouting.

Their importance in the play is twofold: (1) as a chorus expressing feelings aroused by speakers, and a living background to the inter-play of character which is the substance of the drama; (2) a visible force in deciding the fate of the conspirators, which is the counterpart of the invisible force of the supernatural.

One may suspect other than dramatic reasons for this portrayal of the crowd. The attitude of Casca (whose character is Shakespeare's invention) is that of the aristocracy (Roman or Elizabethan). There is more than a suspicion of the 'rabblement' who poured into the pit from the narrow streets across the Thames and clapped or hissed the actors on the stage. It was a lively mob that would line London streets, cheering some noble earl one day as a conquering hero, then hooting him as a traitor before the year was out. Now with cries of encouragement or sympathy ('Alas, good soul!'), now with angry murmurs swelling to a roar ('O traitors, villains!'), their approval or disapproval counted for much. Shakespeare's politics are unknown, but he seems to have shared the aristocrat's contempt for the 'common herd'.

Whether as Commoners downing tools for a triumph or as Citizens voting in the Forum on their country's future, their material enjoyment comes before abstract notions of liberty.

Scene summaries, textual notes and revision questions

Act I
Scene 1

This short introductory scene shows Shakespeare's skill in the use of minor incidents in his original, as do II,4, III,3.

It serves several dramatic purposes.

1 Summarizes recent events.
2 Shows Caesar's growing power.
3 Reveals opposition among the officials of the republic.
4 Anticipates the fickleness of the crowd in forgetting Pompey and in changing their minds under the influence of oratory.

The two tribunes (originally officials elected to defend the interests of the people) here adopt a haughty attitude to the 'vulgar', characteristic of the enmity between aristocrat and plebeian. These partisans of Pompey, in his last days the champion of the Senate, hate the people's new favourite and strike the note which is to be the keynote of the conspiracy – away with 'servile fearfulness'.

The citizens, elsewhere in a dangerous mood, are here seen in a holiday spirit. They are the same Elizabethan crowd that forgives Caesar with all their hearts and cries 'Alas, good soul!' Cockney humour emerges in the chop logic of the cobbler (of the same kin as the Grave-digger in *Hamlet* and the Porter in *Macbeth*), also important as showing that the citizens, while subject to mass emotion as a mob, are as individuals capable of independent thinking. (It is also possible to trace some characterization of the individual citizens in III,2.) Their 'baser metal' is as tongue-tied in shame as, later, they are senseless in indignation.

mechanical Of the working class.

in respect of Compared with.

directly Straight.

naughty Worthless.

recover A pun on 'recover', to restore to health (Elizabethan usage) and 're-cover', to repair (shoes).

neat's Cow's.

What tributaries ... chariot wheels Petty princes appeared in Caesar's previous triumphs. This time he is celebrating victory over other Romans, Pompey's sons defeated in Spain.

You blocks, you stones ... things cf. Antony's speech, III,2,147.

replication Echoing.

Be gone! For other emphatic short lines, cf. I,2,54, II,1,209, V,1,50.

intermit Stop.

most exalted Highest. Note the hyperbole.

metal Disposition. cf. I,2,313.

images Statues (of Caesar).

deck'd with ceremonies Covered with decorations (diadems in Plutarch, scarfs in I,2,289).

the feast of Lupercal It was the custom during the Lupercalia, held on 15 February, in honour of Pan, the shepherd god of fertility, for youths to run naked through the streets whipping those they met with thongs of goat-skin. It would be characteristic of Antony to play a part so out of keeping with the dignity of consul and to take advantage of the festival spirit by trying 'how the people take' the half-playful crowning of Caesar.

the vulgar The common people.

These growing feathers ... pitch A metaphor from the popular Elizabethan sport of falconry.

Scene 2

Caesar's first appearance is one of pomp and ceremony, with a retinue of obsequious flatterers, but a mysterious warning creates the first feeling of suspense in the minds of the audience.

Private discussion alternates with public ceremony. Varied reactions are shown to the god-like behaviour of the dictator: the determined Cassius hates him more with every word he utters; the troubled Brutus is more disturbed by the distant shouts than by anything his friend has to say; the flippant Casca treats both Caesar and the crowd with bored contempt.

Peace ho! Casca, afterwards the first to strike a blow, is here foremost among Caesar's adulators (cf. line 14), or is he already mocking at the 'foolery'?

To touch Calpurnia Caesar's obvious regret at the lack of an heir is an appropriate opening to the scene.

Beware the ides of March The fifteenth. This famous warning, uttered at the Lupercalia, 15 February, is made, by condensation of the plot, to apply to the following day!

the order of the course The running as arranged (probably by the priests).

quick spirit Liveliness, frivolity.

you bear ... hand Metaphor from riding.

Your friend that loves you Cassius's frequent protestations indicate the warmth of his affection. He is a good lover and a bad hater.

veil'd my look, Made my looks a 'veil' to my thoughts.

the trouble of my countenance The mental worry that my face would otherwise show.

Vexed I am ... difference Brutus has been anxious, before being approached by Cassius, about the threat to republican freedom by a man who has shown him great favour.

Passions Feelings.

some soil ... behaviours Grounds for my attitude.

construe any further Take otherwise.

By means whereof ... value i.e. until this explanation he has kept back ideas he would have liked to communicate to Brutus.

shadow Reflection (of your true self).

respect Respected men.

immortal Is this a customary epithet or irony?

modesty Moderately, to some extent.

jealous on Suspicious of.

ordinary Hackneyed.

hold me dangerous In the preceding lines Cassius has drawn a portrait of Antony (at this moment offering the crown to Caesar) without mentioning his name. Later he is to warn Brutus of the danger latent in such a man.

What means this shouting? Cassius's arguments are punctuated by sounds of applause which, though their real meaning is the opposite of Brutus's fears, serve to reinforce those arguments. On each occasion Brutus's remark gives Cassius a cue.

I would not, Cassius; yet I love him well The theme of his soliloquy in II,1.

indifferently With composure.

outward favour Facial features as distinct from inner motives.

controversy Contesting (either with each other or the torrent).

Æneas Legendary ancestor of the Romans, who carried his father from the sack of Troy and reached Italy after years of wandering.

from their colour A pun on military colours.

speeches The only reference to any of Caesar's many accomplishments.

So get the start ... palm alone Metaphors from racing.

Colossus A statue that bestrode the entrance to the harbour of Rhodes, now lost.

Men at some time ... fates Brutus throws the same argument back at him in IV,3,218–19.

Brutus and Caesar Appealing to the republican belief in equality.

conjure with 'em There is some vain conjuring in V,4.

start a spirit Caesar's ghost, however, was quite unlooked for.

Rome ... room Cassius's puns are bitter. cf. ll.95 and 122.

As easily as a king Their assumption that Caesar has been crowned causes them some surprise at the embarrassment shown by Caesar's train.

There was a Brutus once Lucius Junius Brutus, popularly assumed to be the ancestor of Marcus, expelled the tyrannical Tarquins from Rome and became one of the first two consuls in 509 BC. He was famed for his republican zeal, executing his two sons for their share in a royalist revolt. cf. II,1,53–4.

brook'd Allowed.

That you do love me The artificially balanced phrases of this passage are more fully developed in the prose of Brutus's speech in III,2. Antony pretended to admire this kind of oratory (III,2,221).

nothing jealous Not at all in doubt.

aim Guess.

villager Provincial without Roman citizenship.

my weak words cf. Antony's similar depreciation of his own eloquence.

pluck Casca by the sleeve Cassius knows this man.

well given Of a good disposition.

scorn'd his spirit that could be moved Despised his own mind for being moved.

a greater than themselves cf. Cassius's pigmy view of the Colossus in ll.136–8.

I am Caesar ... this ear is deaf Confirmation of Cassius's remark, 'this man is now become a god'.

hooted Shouted (itself another onomatopoeic word).

I know not what you mean by that The 'falling sickness' means something different to each of the three speakers: Casca takes it mockingly as asphyxiation, Brutus literally as Caesar's infirmity, Cassius metaphorically as submission to tyranny.

the players in the theatre Shakespeare has several references to the stage in his plays. He himself trod the boards and probably smelt the breath of the pit. cf. II,1,226 and III,1,111–14.

occupation Trade. Caesar's offer was not made to the aristocracy.

if Caesar had stabbed their mothers The mob was not so complacent after the stabbing of Caesar.

it was Greek to me i.e. 'double-Dutch'. What was probably a quotation by Cicero would be lost on Casca.

foolery Brutus's attitude to the dictatorship is one of patriotic misgivings, Cassius's of personal jealousy, Casca's of ribald disgust.

Will you dine with me tomorrow? Cassius meets Casca returning from the promised supper the same night (see Sc.3) and says what he has to say then.

blunt Dull.

quick mettle Of an intelligent disposition. cf. the spelling in 1.313.

to digest his words Did Casca mean to convey anything in his description? And how was Cassius aware of a real Casca who would be useful in a conspiracy?

'tis meet ... likes Cassius admits the wrong that he is doing to the character of Brutus.

He should not humour me He would not succeed in converting me to his opinion.

obscurely i.e. 'Shall Rome, etc.' (II,1,46–8).

Scene 3

One night passes, a night terrible in portents. The thunder and lightning and wonders fill the blasé Casca with a new respect and provide the gloomy Cassius with a fresh conception of Caesar.

The storm continues through the second Act, though in Scene 1 there is, as it were, a lull in the storm, the black night merely making the plans of the conspirators even blacker; then, once more, in Scene 2, the wrath of the elements adds further dissuasion to that of Calpurnia.

The scene provides sympathetic background and conveys the sense of time elapsing between the prophecy and the day of its fulfilment.

brought you Caesar home? This leaves no doubt that in our play the day before the Ides of March is the Feast of Lupercal!

Are not you mov'd The philosopher Cicero prefers to remain unmoved.

sway Balance.

anything more wonderful Anything else worthy of note.

portentous things Omens.

climate Place.

A Roman But Casca does not deceive the quick ear of Cassius.

what night What a (terrible) night! Not a reference to the calendar.

A very pleasing night to honest men i.e. dark enough for the purposes of men who are on the right side. cf. ll.128–9.

thunderstone Thunderbolt.

I did present myself ... of it Cassius makes his appeal to Brutus an intellectual plea for freedom and equality, but his appeal to Casca is the desperate cry of one who prefers suicide to bondage.

fool Do silly things (verb).

calculate Foretell (from signs).

Why all these things ... quality Why all these things are turned from their true character and ordinary capacities to abnormal behaviour.

the lion in the Capitol Is this Casca's surly beast, or is Shakespeare thinking of the zoo, chiefly lions and bears, kept at the Tower of London from the time of Henry III to 1834?

sufferance Patient endurance (of the yoke).

be retentive to Hold in.

worldly bars i.e. human flesh.

know all the world Let all the world know.

That part ... bear The tyranny as it affects me.

cancel Here 'bond' has the double meaning of 'chains' and 'document'.

with haste As quickly as possible.

So vile a thing as Caesar! Is this a carefully calculated climax like Antony's 'bloody treason' (III,2,196) or an uncontrollable outburst?

indifferent Of no importance.

fleering Grinning (in triumph).

Be factious Stir up others (into revolt).

certain A redundant word.

Of honourable-dangerous consequence Whose result will be honour or death.

Pompey's porch A porch of a hundred marble columns extended in front of the great theatre built a few years previously by Pompey to hold thousands of spectators and hundreds of lions, a not inconsiderable factor in his popularity. This colonnade was a favourite resort by day; by night there would be dark corners in which 'honest men' could foregather.

complexion of the element Colour of the sky.

favour Aspect.

all this done A difficult feat for an hour or two, but such incongruity is not noticed in the development of the plot.

may but find it Cannot help finding it.

the man entire cf. II,1,56 and 112.

countenance Approval.

conceited Expressed.

Revision questions on Act I

1 Describe (a) a Roman triumph, (b) Roman superstitions.

2 Write a character-sketch of Caesar as Cassius sees him.

3 Give as detailed an account as you can of what happened at the Feast of the Lupercal.

Act II

Scene 1

In this scene Brutus makes the fatal decision. A servile Senate is about to crown Caesar. Though this crown would be worn only outside Italy, and though Caesar's conduct seems blameless to Brutus, he fears the great man's *ambition*. The ambitious generally change in character, the higher they ascend. The gentle Brutus foresees a tyrannical Caesar.

The abuse of greatness is, when it disjoins
Remorse from power.

He does not foresee the remorseless vengeance of the triumvirate.

The soliloquy summarises the 'passions of some difference' that have been troubling his mind. His mind is now made up and he finds several things to confirm his decision to kill Caesar.

1 His theory that a crowned Caesar may work mischief.

2 The written appeals to him in person to strike a blow
for freedom.

3 The significance of the Ides of March as Caesar's coronation day
and the day of warning from the gods.

4 The arrival at his house of men of the 'best respect'.

A mere aside – no words are necessary for the audience – is sufficient
to secure his acceptance of the leadership and, having accepted it,
he imposes his honesty on his followers. Delighted at his success,
Cassius raises no objection to the omission of the oath and the exclusion
of Cicero, but the exemption of Antony raises the first of those protests
which eventually lead, in a critical hour, to open quarrel.

The conspirators are carefully identified, as also later when received
by Caesar (II,3) and greeted by Antony (III,1).

orchard Garden.
by the progress of the stars i.e. the storm has obscured them.
Get Put.
the general The general good.
would be Wants to be.
brings forth Hatches.
craves Requires.
do danger Do harm (an old meaning).
affections Feelings.
proof Experience.
round Rung.
base degrees Lower steps.
lest he may, prevent cf. V,1,105, where Brutus the philosopher refuses to
   kill himself 'for fear of what might fall', only to change his mind.
bear no colour for the thing he is Have no justification in the light of his
   present character.
Fashion it thus Express our case in this way.
augmented i.e. with the addition of royal power.
extremities Extremes.
serpent's egg Harking back to his original comparison (1.14).
Is not to-morrow ... March Brutus is thinking of the soothsayer's
   warning. See I,2,19.
calendar Recently reformed by his intended victim.

exhalations Meteors.

My ancestors ... king Echoing, unconsciously perhaps, Cassius's reminder (I,2,159).

Since Cassius first did whet me This implies several sleepless nights, instead of one (and that the present one); Shakespeare's purposes over-rode minor chronological inaccuracies!

motion Movement.

phantasma Nightmare.

The genius ... council A man's guardian spirit disputes with his impulses whether he is to think of his own safety or to act.

insurrection Upheaval.

your brother Cassius Cassius is married to Junia, Brutus's sister.

moe More.

discover Recognize.

mark of favour Feature.

Hide it in smiles and affability Brutus's lofty scorn becomes practical advice in ll.223–6.

path, thy native semblance on Walk about looking as you really are.

Erebus The son of Chaos, in classical mythology. The name signifies darkness, and was therefore, as here, applied to the dark and gloomy space under the earth, through which the shades passed into Hades.

dim Dark.

Decius Brutus Historically Decimus (Decius in Plutarch) was as important in the conspiracy as his namesake Marcus. He had been named next heir after Octavius.

Here lies the east The conspirators, having found their leader, are now preoccupied with a necessary preliminary to any Roman conspiracy – the swearing-in facing east.

fret Eat into.

growing on the south Farther to the south. Inaccurate, as in March the sunrise would be nearly due east.

weighing Considering.

as the Capitol 'Does' omitted. An appropriate addition, in view of the projected assassination. Spectators in the Globe would probably think of the Tower of London to the east of them, the scene of notable executions.

Give me your hands ... one Brutus has 'yielded' and immediately begins to go against the advice of Cassius with his characteristic show of lofty reasons.

the face of men i.e. the shame in men's expressions while they endure Caesar.

idle Empty.

high-sighted Ambitious.

range Metaphor from falconry.

honesty to honesty Misjudgement of his fellow-conspirators.

cautelous Timid through excessive caution.

carrions Used contemptuously, like 'mutton-heads'.

even Steady.

insuppressive Insuppressible.

or ... or Either ... or.

Is guilty of a several bastardy i.e. every drop becomes base blood, un-Roman.

Will purchase us a good opinion Apparently the conspirators cannot borrow enough respectability. cf. I,3,158. 'Purchase' makes a pun of 'silver'.

break with Inform.

his means Antony was Caesar's fellow-consul. Immediately after the assassination he fled to Caesar's house and took possession of his papers, including the will.

Our course will seem too bloody Brutus fondly believes the people will honour them for moderation. cf. ll.179–80.

Let us be sacrificers but not butchers The gentle Brutus abhors the shedding of blood. To him the assassination is a patriotic necessity, not an act of revenge for personal injuries ('necessary and not envious'). He gives the attempt on Caesar's life an almost sacred aspect.

carve ... hew The conspirators' daggers actually met in the body of their victim!

And after seem to chide 'em Anger should cease when its object is attained. For this cooling-off, so characteristic of Brutus, cf. IV,3,112–13.

that were much he should He is hardly likely to do that.

main opinion Personal conviction. Cassius himself is to revert to superstition (V,1,78).

ceremonies Omens.

apparent That have appeared.

augurers 'Augurs' were priestly interpreters of omens. This anticipates the next scene.

unicorns The hunters of these fabulous animals would stand in front of trees and then side-step them.

glasses Mirrors.

toils Snares.

humour Disposition. Decius's influence is seen at work in the next scene.

He loves me well and I have given him reasons The usual relationship of Brutus with his friends: affectionate admiration on their part, philosophic lectures on his. Or it may mean, 'I have given him good reason (cause) to love me'.

fashion Mould.

put on Wear, i.e. show.

our Roman actors See note on 'the players in the theatre', p.41.

weak condition Probably the fever brought on, according to Plutarch, by her self-inflicted wound.

ungently ... ungentle Unusual for Brutus, whose gentleness had just prevented him from waking Lucius.

humour (Temporary) disposition. cf. 1.210.

physical Curative.

sick offence Cause of sickness.

Am I yourself? cf. 1.273

in sort or limitation In a partial or restricted sense.

Cato Marcus Cato Uticensis, 'whom Brutus studied most to follow of all the other Romaines' (Plutarch). Father of the Cato in Act V and doubly related to Brutus, being brother of the latter's mother as well as father of his wife Portia. He was a keen republican and a Stoic, committing suicide at Utica sooner than surrender to Caesar.

Think you I am no stronger than my sex Yet that very weakness is to be illustrated in her. cf. II,4,39.

charactery Writing.

mortified Dead.

Scene 2

Suspense is now mounting. Will Caesar come to the Capitol? Will the conspiracy be betrayed?

We are shown Caesar hiding his fear and the conspirators hiding their intentions.

Another wife is on her knees, but her request is no sooner granted than Caesar is made to feel ashamed of yielding. He blames her fears for yielding, but note what seems dramatic irony at 1.37,

> death, a necessary end,
> Will come when it will come.
> What say the augurers?

He is persuaded to go by Decius's contradictory interpretation of the dr   and, still more, by the news of an intended coronation. Cal-   dream is only too well fulfilled in III,1,105–7.

, the decoy, enters first alone, holding as he does the confi-   Caesar. Later the rest of the band are received courteously.   t the asides of Trebonius and Brutus.

present Immediate.

stood on ceremonies Relied on omens.

one within Stage expression for someone waiting outside! '*Who*' is understood before 'besides'.

most horrid sights Described for the third time! Note the onomatopoeia, especially ll.19 and 22.

beyond all use Quite contrary to custom.

in shame of cowardice To put cowardice to shame.

humour See note p.46.

tonight Last night.

like a fountain Had Shakespeare in mind a contemporary fountain in Cheapside, spouting wine on special occasions?

For tinctures ... cognizance Probably Decius is not too clear what he means. The first three words might apply, strangely enough, to the blood and bones of a martyr, the last means some kind of memento taken from the dead. None of them is appropriate to a fountain of honour!

proceeding Actions.

liable In accordance.

Antony, that revels long o' nights 'In the day-time he would sleepe or walke out his drunkennesse, thinking to weare away the fume of the abundance of wine which he had taken over night' (Plutarch).

like i.e. the same in outward appearance.

yearns Grieves. The hypocrisy of this encounter (invented by Shakespeare) has not been to the liking of Brutus.

Scene 3

The conspiracy does not go unsuspected, but it is fated to succeed (1.16). A vital document shows inside information, but not through any deliberate betrayal.

virtue cannot live ... emulation Virtue always meets with envious hostility.

Scene 4

The soothsayer is an unfortunate choice for Portia to question. His fears serve to increase hers. This scene not only fills the interval between Caesar's departure from his house and his arrival at the Capitol, but is a fine piece of characterization.

rumour Distant noise.

Suit ... befriend himself Is there confusion with Artemidorus?

prætors Judges in civil law. Brutus and Cassius were among them.

void Empty of people.

how weak ... is See note on 'Think you I am no stronger than my sex', p.47.

Revision questions on Act II

1 How does Brutus justify to himself the murder of Caesar?

2 What arguments does Portia use to try to persuade her husband to share his secret with her?

3 Analyse Caesar's reactions to omens and predictions.

Act III

Scene 1

The climax. The entry of Antony's servant is the turning point; that of Octavius's servant makes the removal of the body from the Elizabethan stage easier.

Instead of subsiding after Caesar's death, interest is maintained by the meeting of Antony with the conspirators, which begins the conflict that continues to the end of the play.

Caesar's manner becomes more overbearing, that of his assailants more obsequious as the fatal moment approaches.

Anxiety on the part of the audience for the conspirators becomes anxiety for Antony.

Antony's eloquent emotion should have been a warning to Brutus. It is almost a rehearsal of his public oration.

What, is the fellow mad? The 'public conscience' has done his best to get a hearing.

Casca, be sudden This reference is made clearer to the audience in 1.30.

prevent Anticipate (in the matter of your brother).

the law of children i.e. the rules of childish games are soon altered.

fond Foolish.

enfranchisement Re-admission to citizenship.

If I could pray to move i.e. if there were any higher authority than myself that could be moved by my prayers (cf. the reference to the Pole Star in the next line).

no fellow in the firmament No equal in the sky.

apprehensive Able to reason or imagine. This line is parallel to l.64; 'flesh and blood' correspond to 'fire', as 'apprehensive' to 'shine'.

That unassailable ... motion Who because he is immune to attack, keeps his position, and is not thrown off his course.

et tu, Brute 'and you, Brutus'.

mutiny Insurrection.

stand upon Think about, cf. II,2,13.

bathe our hands in Caesar's blood cf. Calpurnia's dream, related, II,2,76–9.

bleed in sport i.e. on the stage. See also note on 'the players in the theatre', p.41.

on Pompey's basis The scene of the murder has been transferred by Shakespeare to the Capitol from a court-house off Pompey's Theatre in the Campus Martius a good half mile away. With it he has taken Pompey's statue (see note on 'Pompey's porch', p.43).

'Caesar ... was driven either casually or purposedly, by the counsel of the conspirators, against the base whereupon Pompey's image stood which ran all of a goare bloud till he was slaine' (Plutarch).

be resolv'd Have it explained. cf. III,2,183.

untrod state New conditions.

falls shrewdly to the purpose i.e. his doubts still hold good (cf. II,1,183).

rank Overgrown.

bear ... hard Have a spite against.

purpled With red dye.

no mean of death No method of execution.

The choice and master spirits of this age Is this the first example of Antony's irony?

Our hearts ... Caesar Brutus speaks for himself.

malice Probably a misprint for 'welcoe', abbreviation of 'welcome'.

appeased Calmed.

conceit Look on.

sign'd in thy spoil Marked (for what they are, like the artisans of 1,1) in your blood. 'Spoil' has here the sense of something broken open by cutting or digging, *not* the trophies of victory.

lethe The intended meaning is 'life-blood'. Lethe was one of the rivers of the underworld of death.

cold modesty Moderate language. cf. similar depreciation of his eloquence in III,2,227–8.

prick'd in number Ticked off on a list. cf. IV,1,1.

Therefore i.e. in order to join you.

so full of good regard So well considered.

moreover The bomb-shell is introduced as an after-thought.

protest Declare.

speak all good A loop-hole of which Antony is to make good use.

the tide of times The meaning is uncertain. cf. IV,3,218.

hand Which particular hand is Antony thinking of?

A curse shall light ... men Other limbs than Caesar's shall be mangled.

domestic fury Civil war had ravaged Italy several times previously, but Shakespeare often puts prophetic utterances into the mouths of his characters.

in use Customary.

Até Roman goddess of discord and revenge.

confines Territories.

'Havoc.' 'No quarter.'

Passion Emotion.

issue Handiwork.

Scene 2

The scene shifts from the Capitol, deserted by a panic-stricken Senate, to the Forum, thronged with enquiring Citizens. 'Ambition's debt is paid'; the cause of freedom is now on its trial. The dead man prided himself on his constancy; no such quality is found in those who first applaud Brutus the liberator and then break loose to avenge Caesar the benefactor. The blame for fickleness, however, is not entirely theirs. The first occupant of the pulpit not only chooses to play his innings first, but does not wait to see that the restrictions he has imposed are observed. He even refuses to leave Antony without an audience.

First Citizen   We'll bring him to his house
　　　　　　　With shouts and clamours.
Brutus   Good countrymen, let me depart alone,
　　　　　And, for my sake, stay here with Antony.

Would not Cassius have marched off the scene in triumph? In a very short time the same citizen cries,

We'll burn the house of Brutus.

Brutus's appeal to reason is convincing in its logic, but its reception is that of a crowd already in the grip of mob excitement. Their applause, too, is a denial of all that Brutus has endangered his life for. Let Brutus be Caesar, with a crown, a statue and a triumph! In face of such applause Antony begins cautiously, but Caesar's achievements are good arguments and Caesar's will an irresistible weapon, cunningly wielded. Material benefits come home more surely than the call to freedom.

It is, however, when Caesar's body, with its twenty-three wounds, is uncovered that the mob begins to get out of hand. The sight of their mangled favourite makes them forget the terms of his will. Caesar's dead body drives Brutus out of Rome to meet his spirit at Philippi.

This scene is remarkable in that the speeches and their effects are even more dramatic than the assassination itself. The speeches contrast sharply: Brutus's has the prose rhythm suitable to the orator's devices, Antony's the verse rhythm which moves the emotions with its imagination, irony, pathos and hatred. Brutus argues down to the people, Antony identifies himself with them; Brutus explains the honourable character of his action, Antony mourns his friend, *their* friend.

That other audience, the spectators in the theatre, is similarly moved; the exclamations of the Citizens give expression to their feelings also.

question Case.

extenuated Lessened.

enforced Exaggerated.

beholding Obliged, beholden.

I come to bury Caesar ... bones These famous lines might be paraphrased thus: Caesar will be remembered for his bad ambition, which caused him to be assassinated; he had good qualities, however, and these I mean to touch on before they are buried with him for ever.

I thrice presented him This is the only one of the four points at all relevant to ambition, but all appealed to the popular mind.

O judgment! Seeing that he has the crowd with him, Antony lets himself go.

none so poor Antony is the sole official mourner.

honourable men The irony in 1.156 is now patent to the meanest intellect.

the Nervii A warlike tribe of the Belgae. The Romans snatched victory out of imminent defeat.

be resolv'd See note p.50.

most unkindest The best-known example of a double superlative.

dint of pity Touch of compassion.

I know not Did Brutus acquaint Antony with his reasons 'so full of good regard'?

with reasons A scornful allusion to Brutus.

I only speak right on But Antony's speech is as cunningly developed as Brutus's is elaborately logical.

drachmas Coins worth about one-tenth of a pound.

We'll burn his body, etc 'For some of them cryed out, Kill the murtherers: others plucked up forms, tables, and stalles about the market place . . . and having laid them all on a heape together, they set them on fire, and thereupon did put the body of Caesar, and burnt it in the midst of the most holy places. And furthermore, when the fire was thoroughly kindled, some here, some there, tooke burning firebrands, and ran with them to the murtherers houses that killed him, to set them afire. Howbeit, the conspirators forseeing the daunger before, had wisely provided for themselves, and fledde' (Plutarch).

upon a wish In answer to my unspoken wish.

Some notice of the people i.e. some signs of disturbance or shouting.

are rid Have ridden.

Scene 3

This scene shows not only the ugly temper of the mob, but the unreasonableness of their fury. It also adds a touch of comic relief. See also p.37.

things unluckily charge my fantasy My mind is loaded with ideas that are full of bad omens.

Revision questions on Act III

1 How does Caesar meet the petition for the recall of Publius Cimber?

2 What have you noticed about Brutus's attitude to Caesar alive, Caesar dead, Antony, the Citizens?

3 Why did Brutus leave the Forum alone?

4 Attempt a character-sketch of the Fourth Citizen, based on his remarks in Scenes 2 and 3.

Act IV

Scene 1

The 'butchers' have replaced the 'sacrificers'. The extent of the proscription is revealed in Sc.3, ll.173–80. Cicero is not mentioned here, but he was Octavius's contribution. Octavius requires Lepidus to give up his brother, Lepidus requires Antony to give up his nephew (altered from uncle), but Antony's spite against Cicero for the speeches the latter had made against him is omitted. Perhaps Shakespeare thought that for Octavius to yield to Antony would be out of keeping with his obstinate character in the play (cf. V,1,20).

Is Antony's treatment of Lepidus due to resentment at Lepidus's requiring the life of his nephew or simply greed for more power? Lepidus remained in charge in Rome while the other two prosecuted the campaign against the republicans.

The reference to the will makes this scene appear to follow naturally on the last, though actually the gap was eighteen months and the meeting was in North Italy. cf. also III,2,270.

damn Condemn.
Caesar's house An error, since Antony went to join the others there (III,2,269).
charge Expenses. Caesar was too generous!
slight Worthless. cf. IV,3,37.
To ease ... loads To save ourselves from slanderous accusations of seizing too much for ourselves.
wind Turn.
abject Things thrown away by others.
orts Scraps.
property Piece of furniture.
Our best friends ... stretch'd Our friends enlisted on our side and our resources fully exploited. The line is three syllables short.

How covert matters ... disclos'd How to find out hidden snags.
at the stake A metaphor from bear-baiting.

Scene 2

Brutus and Cassius meet after a long interval, in which they have been raising forces in separate provinces. (They were fortunate in enlisting large numbers from Pompey's discharged soldiers and dissatisfied princes). There is no word of this in the play. It is the clash between their characters that has dramatic importance.

There seems to be an error in the stage direction, Lucilius and Titinius changing places. Brutus, accompanied by Titinius and soldiers, meets Lucilius, returning from seeing Cassius, together with Cassius's slave, Pindarus.

change i.e. of attitude.
familiar instances Signs of close friendship.
enforced See note p.52.
hot at hand Reined in.
Stand! Stand! Stand! A stage device to convey the impression of a large
  army.
wrong I mine enemies? 'Taking all the small towns and villages, he did
  let all the prisoners he tooke, go without payment of ransome, hoping by
  this his great courtesie to win them' (Plutarch).
content Quiet.
Lucilius, do you the like Probably an error for Lucius. It would be more
  appropriate for him to take a message, similar to that of his fellow-slave
  Pindarus. Then Lucilius would be on guard with his fellow-officer Titinius,
  as he is when the Poet thrusts his way in. Lucius would naturally return
  and be in attendance. 'Lucius' is also more suited to the scansion.

Scene 3

In this scene the incompatibility of temperament between Brutus and Cassius reaches its climax. Lofty motive confronts practical expediency. The love of freedom which aimed at killing Caesarism is matched with the lust for power which struck the blow at Caesar himself.

The quarrel is dramatic not only in its subtle contrast of character, but in that it threatens to disrupt the republican forces in time of danger and that the reconciliation dignifies the two men just before their final farewell.

We are given a full-length portrait of Brutus: his lofty principle and the moral scruples that lead him into contradictions, his rigid philosophy with its display of well-considered reasons and its stoic indifference to grief, his devotion to books and music and his intolerance of moral or intellectual inferiority ('Away, slight man!' 'Saucy fellow, hence!'), his gentleness and consideration for others, his calm temperament ruffled by one of those rare outbursts of temper that are soon over, yet quite unruffled by a ghost, and that confidence in his own judgement which leads him to commit the last fatal blunder.

The intrusion of the poet seems to have no purpose, unless it is intended as comic relief. It may be merely the result of following Plutarch closely. A more sinister explanation might be the rough treatment handed out to poets in this play!

The 'evil spirit' of Brutus is made by Shakespeare to appear in the form of Caesar's ghost, the ghost of his benefactor. Its appearance is a return to the supernatural element which overshadowed the beginning of the play. Caesar *himself* is now an omen.

Music, rarely absent from a Shakespearean play, here has a soothing effect after the passions that have been aroused and induces that rapt stillness which is the best preliminary to a ghostly visitation.

noted Literally branded: made an example of.
nice Petty.
bear his comment Be criticised.
mart Market.
And chastisement . . . head i.e. others escape punishment with you as an example.
villain Prolepsis: such a man would be a villain.
supporting robbers There is a reference in Plutarch, to Antony among others: 'Now it grieved men much, to see that Caesar should be out of Italy . . . and that others in the meane time abusing his name and authority, should commit such insolent and outragious parts unto their citizens . . . many extortions, cruelties and robberies' (Plutarch).
mighty space Contrasted with a handful of gold.
large honours Great offices we can bestow. Brutus's self-importance is seen also in V,1,60. His comparisons, too, at this time are strange, possibly because of a distracted mind.

older in practice 'Now Cassius would have done Brutus as much honour, as Brutus did unto him: but Brutus most commonly prevented him, and went first unto him, both because he was the elder man, as also for that he was sickly of body. And men reputed him commonly to be very skilful in warres, but otherwise marvellous chollericke and cruell, who sought to rule men by feare, rather than with lenitie' (Plutarch).

Have mind upon your health As you value your life.

slight See note, p.54.

Digest the venom of your spleen Keep your temper down.

respect Heed.

For I can raise no money by vile means. 'Cassius . . . after he had compelled the Rhodians everie man to deliver all the ready money they had in gold and silver in their houses, the which being brought together, amounted to the summe of eight thousand talents: yet he condemned the citie besides, to pay the sum of five hundred talents more. Where Brutus in contrarie manner, after he had levied of all the country of Lycia but a hundred and fiftie talents onely: he departed thence into the countrie of Ionia, and did them no more hurt'' (Plutarch).

indirection Crooked methods.

for gold to pay my legions. However it may have been extorted!

Olympus The Greek mountain, where the gods lived; cf. III, line 74.

brav'd Defied.

check'd Rebuked.

Plutus Better Pluto's. Pluto was king of the underworld.

humour State of mind, disposition. cf. line 120.

hasty spark cf. 'show of fire', I,2, 176–7, and see note on 'And after seem to chide 'em', p.46.

more years This makes the dispute in ll.31–4 seem childish now.

cynic Philosopher.

fashion Way of speaking.

Companion Fellow.

That tidings News of her death and of the Caesarian preparations arrived together. cf. 1.167.

swallow'd fire 'She determining to kill herselfe (her parents and friends carefully looking to her to keepe her from it) tooke hote burning coles and cast them into her mouth, and kept her mouth so close, that she choked her selfe' (Plutarch).

art i.e. philosophy in theory, as distinct from putting it into practice. Cassius was an Epicurean, Brutus a Stoic.

alive Let the dead bury their dead.

marching to Philippi From Sardis in Asia Minor to Philippi in Macedonia took them from spring to November, 42 BC. The swift action of the play, however, carries the spectator by a natural transition to the plains of Philippi, the scene of Act V.

in a forc'd affection Loyal to us only because they are compelled to be.

new-added Increased by recent recruitment.

There is a tide ... ventures See note on 'Men at some time ... fates', p.40.

Which we will niggard i.e. grudge her a niggardly hour or two.

o'er-watch'd Awake too long.

mace A 'murderous' weapon. 'Leaden' suggests the heaviness of sleep. cf. 'honey-heavy dew of slumber', II,1,230.

leaf The Romans used rolls, not books.

How ill this taper burns! Ghostly influence.

stare Stand erect.

Thy evil spirit It is curious that having turned the mysterious phantom of history into the ghost of Caesar, Shakespeare, who wrote long speeches for the ghost of Hamlet's father, should have given it no more to say than Plutarch gives! However, the supernatural intervention, taciturn as it is, intensifies the sense of impending tragedy and electrifies the audience.

Revision questions on Act IV

1 What part in the Triumvirate does Antony intend Lepidus to play?

2 What two reasons restrain Brutus from raising money by corrupt methods?

3 In how many ways does Brutus anger Cassius?

4 Who is more to blame in the quarrel scene?

Act V

Scene 1

This is a gloomy act, full of farewell speeches and impromptu funeral orations, though full of entertainment in the hurry and rush of the short scenes, the alarums, shouts and stabs.

The taunts of Scene 1 are Shakespeare's addition, in the manner of his English histories. It balances the opposing sides and brings the four main characters into contrast.

For the first and only time, a word from Cassius causes Brutus to change his mind about suicide and forsake his philosophy in order to shield his honour (or does he hope, vainly, to slay or be slain?).

After the appearance of Caesar's ghost, Brutus is oppressed by a fatalist feeling that his end is near. Cassius has turned superstitious and in Scene 3, carrying out his oft-uttered threat, kills himself, through a misunderstanding, in the hour of Brutus's victory. A noble instinct makes him conceal these superstitious fears from Brutus (l.94), but both now anticipate the worst.

our hopes are answered This does not refer to Brutus's decision in the last scene, as it might seem to do. Nevertheless, his impatience to 'know the end' has obviously led him to forsake a better strategic position, as later he gives the command to charge too soon.

battles Battalions.

warn Summon.

fearful bravery Formidable array. 'Brutus' army was inferior to Octavius Caesar, in number of men: but for bravery and rich furniture, Brutus' army far excelled Caesar's' (Plutarch).

Upon the right hand I This change-over is made by Shakespeare. Not only was Octavius sick, but Cassius yielded again (in Plutarch) to Brutus, letting him have the *right* wing opposite Octavius. In the play, however, Brutus (L.) overcomes Octavius (R.), and Cassius (R.) is overcome by Antony (L.).

exigent Emergency.

I do not cross you; but I will do so This is the only hint Shakespeare lets fall of the division between Octavius and Antony, of which he had read so much and which he was to incorporate some years later in *Antony and Cleopatra*. As rival armies are best represented on the stage by their leaders, our dramatist restores Octavius not only to health, but to a position of equal importance with the others, whereas, in Plutarch, 'Caesar did no great matter, but Antonius had alway the upper hand, and did all'.

The student may be left to decide for himself whether this intriguing line means (1) I am not deliberately thwarting you, but I am going to cross over to the other wing, or (2) I shall not go against your wishes *now*, but I shall do later on.

countrymen Brutus is the only one to think of his enemies as compatriots.

The posture of your blows are yet unknown Your method of attack is yet to be revealed. 'Are' is due to attraction, the verb agreeing erroneously with the nearest noun.

honeyless. stingless. soundless The meaning of these verbal hits is not easy to follow: perhaps to Cassius Antony's words are bitter enough to destroy all the honey of Hybla; Antony suggests that he has taken their stings as well; Brutus retorts that if he has done so, he has also acquired the bees' habit of buzzing first.

Hybla A mountain in Sicily, covered with fragrant flowers, making the local honey famous.

You show'd your teeth ... neck Antony was not an eye-witness, but his imagination made up for it, as in III,2,178–93.

If Cassius might have rul'd If I had had my way, i.e. in not sparing Antony, in denying him the funeral speech, and in not seeking the enemy forces.

Look The short line emphasizes the pause as he draws his sword.

thou couldst not die more honourable See note on 'large honours', p.56.

stomachs Courage (appetite for fighting).

Why now, blow wind ... bark A desperate state of mind, explained by his remarks to Messala. cf. *Macbeth*, V,5,51, 'Blow wind! come, wrack!'

on the hazard At stake.

Upon one battle all our liberties 'Messala, I protest unto thee and make thee my witnesse, that I am compelled against my mind and will to ieopard the libertie of our countrie, to the hazard of a battell. *And yet we must be lively, and of good corage,* considering our good fortune whom we should wrong too much to mistrust her, although we follow evill counsell' (Plutarch).

Epicurus A Greek philosopher (BC 341–270). The Epicurean ideal was the pleasure of a mind at rest, the Stoic ideal was virtue based on reason, and not on emotion. The one degenerated into self-indulgence, hence *epicurean*, the other became synonymous with 'heroic endurance'. Both schools based human judgement on the physical senses, thus ruling out the supernatural.

credit ... presage Believe in omens.

former Foremost.

ravens cf. *Macbeth*, I,5,37, 'The raven himself is hoarse ...'

Even so Brutus has finished his conversation with Lucilius. This is a dramatic device so that Brutus and Lucilius are not stranded while Cassius and Messala are holding the stage.

stand friendly Belying the doubts just expressed. See the above extract from Plutarch.

blame Cato See note on Cato, p.47.

prevent the time Anticipate the end (by suicide). See also note on 'lest he may, prevent', p.44.

stay the providence Await the fate decreed.

O! that a man might know ... known 'Cassius was of opinion not to try this war at one battell, but rather to delay time, and to draw it out in length, considering that they were the stronger in mony, and the weaker in men and armors. But Brutus in contrary maner, did always before and at that time also, desire nothing more, then to put all to the hazard of battell, as soone as might be possible' (Plutarch).

Scene 2

Brutus's impatiences brings disaster.

This is not the shortest scene in Shakespeare. cf. *Antony and Cleopatra*, IV,11.

Ride, ride, Messala This is the troop discerned by Cassius in Scene 3.
bills Instructions.
the other side Cassius's wing.

Scene 3

Cassius's end is as tragic as that of Brutus. He who has so often seen through things kills himself on a misunderstanding of what he sees, though Shakespeare makes him use the eyes of another.

His birthday has the same fatal obsession for him that the ghost has for Brutus. The manner of his death confirms Brutus's belief that the spirit of Caesar himself is avenging itself on the conspirators.

ensign Standard-bearer.
even with a thought As quickly as thinking. cf. 'upon a wish', p.53.
Parthia In Asia Minor, where Cassius did much to retrieve a heavy Roman defeat.
O my heart! Cassius has just referred to Titinius as his best friend.
misconstrued every thing Cassius has always been right till now.
own proper Very own.
Low alarums Caesar in the background?
moe More.
Thasos A small island in the Aegean, off the coast of Thrace.
a second fight Historically, the second battle, fought twenty days later. Brutus was the only leader to come, with credit, out of the first conflict. 'For Antonius, to flie the furie of the first charge, was gotten in the next marrish: and no man could tell what became of Octavius Caesar, after he was carried out of his campe' (Plutarch).

Scene 4

A snatch of fighting is inserted between the desperate suicides of Cassius and Brutus. It relieves the gloom and gives an opportunity for Lucilius to show *his* devotion to *Brutus*.

Is Antony's desire to take Brutus alive a desire to lead him in triumph through Rome or to honour him in deed as he does in word at the end of the play?

my country's friend Still the liberator. Or should these two lines, given without the name of the speaker in the Folios, be spoken by Lucilius, in preparation for 1.14? '*Exit*' is also omitted in the Folios.

Scene 5

Death brings honour to Brutus, much as it brings final triumph to Caesar.

The audience is kept in suspense wondering whether Brutus will be taken alive or escape the disgrace. Three friends in turn refuse to hold his sword for him, until a slave does so, as a slave did the same office for Cassius. Honour is saved. The republican leaders have both died on their own swords.

Death heals all wounds. The Antony who displayed the 'most unkindest cut of all' to a weeping crowd, who reminded Brutus of the hole he made in Caesar's heart, and who sneered at Brutus's honour and mocked his reasons, now acclaims him 'the noblest Roman of them all'.

The last words are spoken by Caesar's heir and the future master of the Roman world.

poor remains of friends Indicating complete defeat.
the torch-light Suggesting the surrounding darkness.
I know my hour is come cf. the fatalism of Cassius, V,3,25.
entertain Accept into my service.
them all i.e. the conspirators.
in a general ... all Thinking honestly and without private malice of the common good. cf. I,2,85.
call the field to rest Stop the fighting.
part Share.

Revision questions on Act V

1 How many points of dramatic importance can you find in Scene 1?

2 Compare and contrast the deaths of Brutus and Cassius.

3 Write notes on the minor characters in this Act.

General questions

1 Describe Caesar as seen by (*a*) Decius Brutus, (*b*) Marcus Brutus, (*c*) Antony.

2 Do you think that Shakespeare regarded the assassination as a crime, fittingly punished?

3 Give in your own words the substance of the two funeral speeches.

4 How far does the 'spirit' of Caesar influence the course of the drama?

5 Illustrate from the play (*a*) the atmosphere of ancient Rome as created by the dramatist, and (*b*) the limitations imposed by the period in which he lived.

6 What references are made to events and incidents involving Caesar before the opening of the play, and with what purposes are they introduced?

7 Comment on the use of stage humour in this play, and distinguish three different kinds, criticising their suitability for the occasion.

8 Which of the two conspirators, Brutus and Cassius, appeals to you more? Give your reasons.

9 What qualities in Brutus unfitted him for (*a*) conspiracy, (*b*) leadership?

10 How many different acts of revenge can you find in this play?

11 Which two speeches (*a*) exercised most influence on the action, and which two (*b*) revealed most intimately the real characters of the speakers?

12 How did individual conspirators, apart from the two leaders, contribute to the success of the undertaking?

13 Describe in some detail what you consider the best example of (*a*) loyalty, (*b*) treachery.

14 Why do you think Shakespeare gave the citizens a much greater part in the play than the Senate?

15 What would be lost if the women's parts were omitted?

16 Tell the story as Lucius would see it.

17 What changes came over Cassius towards the end?

18 You are dull, Casca, and those sparks of life
That should be in a Roman you do want,
Or else you use not.
Explain this utterance from the immediate circumstances, and compare it with what you know of Casca.

19 What use is made in *Julius Caesar* of (*a*) dreams, (*b*) omens, (*c*) philosophy?

20 Would you agree that destiny seems more overwhelming in this than in any other Shakespeare play?

21 How would you set the stage and group the actors for Act III, Scenes 1 and 2?

22 'A mob is a collective bully made up of individual cowards.' Does this modern definition fit the crowd in *Julius Caesar*? Give your reasons.

23 'Et tu, Brute?' Why do you think this was expressed in Latin? Mention other equally terse and significant phrases, relating them to their contexts.

24 What features make this play especially suitable for film production?

25 'The most splendidly written political melodrama we possess' (G. B. Shaw, by no means biased towards Shakespeare). What lessons has *Julius Caesar* for the twentieth century?